T0162997

SUCCEEDING
by the
WINGS OF
GOD

A masterpiece with divine secrets
for great heights in life

HARRISON I. ENUDI

Order this book online at www.trafford.com
or email orders@trafford.com

Most Trafford titles are also available at major online book retailers.

Printed in the United States of America.

For further information, contact:
DESTINY AWARENESS OUTREACH, SOUTH KOREA.
E-mail: dao@pastorharrisonenudi.org, contact@pastorharrisonenudi.org
Web: www.pastorharrisonenudi.org

ISBN: 978-1-4669-3305-7 (sc)
ISBN: 978-1-4669-3306-4 (e)

Trafford rev. 09/18/2012

 www.trafford.com

North America & international
toll-free: 1 888 232 4444 (USA & Canada)
phone: 250 383 6864 ♦ fax: 812 355 4082

CONTENTS

ACKNOWLEDGEMENT

To God be the glory! God is too faithful to fail! I am really grateful to God for helping me through in making this book a reality today. No divine mission or assignment is achievable by human energy. Every divine assignment demands a divine help for total accomplishment.

I never thought of writing this book; but when the Lord impressed the idea into my spirit, the grace to do it came upon me immediately. He said, "Put all the principles I have thought you all these years concerning achieving divine success without struggle in a book for me". Then, I began the mission of documenting these secrets, which you are about to encounter, as you read through the pages, into this piece.

Indeed, I owe it all to God for His enabling grace to write! Thank you Lord, for making me a pen in your hand unto my generation and the world at large!

INTRODUCTION

Success without struggle is impossible without God. History has proven it from ages that any nation without the true God is perpetually under a curse. There is no failure with God almighty. Check the history of the Jews; you will find out that they are epitome of success because of covenant practices with the almighty God, except when they walk away from the covenant.

The covenant between a man (or Nation) and God is one of God's feathers for a great flight. What do I mean by 'The wings of God'? The wings of God are divine instructions for a wonderful and a glorious flight in the world of success.

Human wisdom is failing virtually in almost every area of life (because it is limited); thereby, leaving doubts in the minds of people. It has left undeniable traces of economic crashes, political malfunctioning, industrial dilapidations, national and international conflicts, unpredicted disasters, the struggles of individual and cooperate bodies or organizations, the decadence of human health worldwide without a lasting solution, and streams of doubt in human philosophies and ideologies.

Until you embrace the different dimensions of God's practical secrets (Ways) for true success, you will remain a byword; struggling to break away from the yoke of unproductive life or the cycle of failure, or you will only achieve the measure of success that human energy can reach. Jesus said, *"I am the way, the truth and the life."* (John 14:6). Also, mathematically, the bible declared Jesus as the word of God (John 1:1-3, 14). It therefore implies that the word of God contains the secrets for finding the different ways to our individual dreamland.

There are no other short cuts to having a sweatless success other than God's ways (Principles). The book of Joshua in the old Testament (Covenant) of the bible tells us that the book of the law (The bible) should not depart out of our mouth (we should keep confessing its truth) and that we should always meditate on its content; for thereby shall we make our ways prosperous and then, we shall have **good success** (Joshua 1:8).

Therefore, this very book in your hand (which you are reading now) is specifically loaded with divine secrets for true success in life and endeavors revealed to me by God to teach humanity. You are so lucky to have a copy today. You cannot go beyond the limit of the natural sphere except by climbing on the wings of our 'Mother-Eagle'-God. No scientist has ever tried it once in this life; not even NASA with all their wealth of scientific knowledge can do that.

It took the power of God for Jesus to break the law of gravity by rising from the grave, overcoming the power of death and hell. Something supernatural is about to happen to your life for good as you read through the pages of this wonderful piece. There is no barrier to divine flight. Jesus, Elisha and Enoch knew this! And you are about to experience it likewise in your life and endeavor. You are about to soar on God's wings, and you will never know failure again in your life. Your last failure is the last you will ever experience. I mean, you are about to leave the realm of human struggle as you consciously flip through the pages of this gracious piece to discover and apply the unfolded divine secrets available in it from divinity. I see you smiling from now!

The creator of life has fast rules to it. Until you work by these rules, you will be ruled out. It is time to give up your human ideology and embrace the manifold wisdom of God almighty. King Nebuchadnezzar, the one-time king of Babylon knew this! King Pharaoh of the 'Egypt' of Moses' days knew this! And it cannot be denied by this generation and the ones to come. The bible says, *"He that wandereth out of the way of understanding shall dwell in the congregation of the dead"* (Proverbs 21:16). New International Version puts it this way, *"Whoever strays from the path of prudence comes to rest in the company of the dead."*

Dead people don't have understanding; only the living does. So many people are dead toward the things of God because God's spirit is lacking in them. This is why it is difficult for them to understand the things that partain to God or the things that God says.

See what God's word says: *"I said days should speak, and multitude of years should teach wisdom. But there is a spirit in man: and the inspiration of the almighty giveth them understanding"* (Job 32:7-8). So, it is not the number of years or wealth of experience that matters, when faced with mysterious event. It is the wisdom of God that will demystify it to your understanding; otherwise, it can sink its victims (you are exempted in Jesus' name)!

You need divine guidance, if you must succeed in this mysterious world. Investors have missed it so many times. Huge amount of money have been lost to several foolish steps. The future of so many families is at stake now because of concurrent economic crises. So many great businesses have gone down the drain because men have neglected the creator of heaven and earth for the pursuit of human ideologies. Remember the case of Paul, the

For he shall be like heath in the desert, and shall not see when good cometh . . ." (Jeremiah 17:5, 6)

Putting your hope in a mortal man could lead you into the hands of frustration. People will make a mess out of your life the moment you make them your god (because they are not meant to be your god). What God has destined your life to be cannot be achieved by depending on the help of man, because humans are limited.

See what a king told a Samaritan woman: *"And as the king of Israel was passing by upon the wall, there cried a woman unto him, saying, Help, my lord, O king. And he said, If the Lord do not help thee, whence shall I help thee?" (2 Kings 6:26, 27).* What an answer! Your help is not in the hand of a mortal man. God is the source of all genuine help, while humans are just divine channels. Set your eyes on Him. He will never fail you!

If what you are asking for has not received answer from God, there is a purpose. Remember, all things works together for good to those that love God, and are called according to His purpose. Sometimes, it is good to seek the will of God concerning our situation than to demand for a change according to our own will. If God had answered the prayers of Jesus in the garden of Gethsemane, salvation would not have been possible today, because it would have been aborted on the altar of prayers. God cannot justify any prayer that attempts to derail His ultimate plan for anyone.

Still on the subject of help: the bible says, *"Woe unto them that go down to Egypt for help, and stay on horses, and trust in chariots, because they are many; and in horsemen, because they are strong; but they look not unto the Holy one of Israel, neither seek the Lord. Now the Egyptians are men, and not God; and their horses flesh, and not spirit. When the Lord shall stretched out his hand, both he that helpeth shall fall, and he that is helped shall fall down, and they shall fail together"* (Isaiah 31:1, 3).

It is even a shameful thing that the Christians put their hope on a non-Christian, all because the non-Christian is financially comfortable or occupying a political position. This is but an absolute absurdity and an insult on the work of redemption. How can a living being put any form of confidence in the dead? It is purely a misconception of hierarchy. No matter what, you are more placed than an unbeliever in Christ; for the bible says, *"A living dog is better than a dead lion"* (Ecclesiastes 9:4).

The respect I have for those that are born again is never to be compared to that of a non-Christian. Relying on an unbeliever for survival gives them room to mock at your Christianity without your knowledge. Sometimes, even before your face, they do it directly or with style. You need a redirection of your mental faculty or a mental transformation to help you think properly, so you will stop disgracing divinity.

See why God blessed Abraham: *"And the king of Sodom said unto Abraham, Give me the persons, and take the goods to thyself. And Abram said to the king of Sodom, I have lifted up mine hand unto the Lord, the most high God, the possessor of heaven and earth. That I will not take from a thread even to a shoelatchet, and that I will not take anything that is not mine, lest thou shouldest say, I have made Abram rich . . . And after these things, the word of the Lord came to Abram in a vision, saying, fear not Abram: I am thy shield, and thy exceeding great reward"* *(Genesis 14:21-23; 15:1)*. You can't show God such a honor and not provoke His heart to lavish His wealth on you. He said, *"I will honor those that honor me" (1 Samuel 2:30B)*. Abraham lived to testify tot this fact as a beneficiary of God's financial honor.

How can we locate the help of God?

Every flow of blessings in the kingdom of God here on earth is the product of the application of divine secrets. There is no one man on earth, in the kingdom of God, that is great, who did not trade on God's covenant secrets. The application of divine secrets is the reason for the manifestation of divine blessings in the life of the applicant.

Looking up to God with an alternative in your heart will never lead you to anywhere but to disappointment. But if you completely depend on God with all your heart, you will surely see His hand move on your behalf for your good.

Let us unveil some of the secrets of God that can help you locate the help of God in your life and endeavor.

1. **Complete trust in God**—*"Trust in the Lord, and do good; so shall thou dwell in the land, and verily thou shall be fed. Delight thyself also in the Lord, and he shall give thee the desire of thine heart. Commit thy ways unto the Lord; trust also in him; and he shall bring it to pass"* (Psalms 37:3-5). It pays to trust the Lord. God will never put those that trust in Him to shame. Remember Daniel in the lion's den! Also, Jesus trusted in his father that he will not leave him in the grave. That is why he accepted to die for humanity; and on the third day, as God promised, he was raised from grave (Luke 24:1-8; Acts 2:25-27).

See what King David said, *"The King shall joy in thy strength, O Lord; and in thy salvation how greatly shall he rejoice! Thou hast given him his heart's desire, and hast not withheld the request of his lips. Selah. For thou preventest him with the blessings of goodness: thou settest a crown of pure gold on his head. He asked life of thee, and thou gavest it him, even length of days forever and ever. His glory is in thy salvation: honour and majesty has thou laid upon him. For thou hast made him most blessed forever: thou has made him exceeding glad with thy countenance.* **For the King trusteth in the Lord . . .** *" (Psalms 21:1-7).*

Trust is one of the most powerful things that woo God into doing the unusual for anyone. *"The Lord is my strength and my shield; my heart trusted in him, and I am helped . . ." (Psalms 28:7).* I see help coming your way speedily!

Again, out of experience, the Psalmist wrote a song in this manner: *"O taste and see that the Lord is good: blessed is the man that trusteth in him" (Psalms 34:8).*

Of all that the Israelites went through, and of all that happened to them on their way to Canaan, from Egypt, The Lord was the one that saw them through every season of their journey, both in the wilderness, desert and before their enemies.

See what the bible said concerning that: *"If it had not been the Lord who was on our side, when men rose up against us: then they had swallowed us up quick, when their wrath was kindled against us. Blessed be the Lord, who had not given us as a prey to their teeth. Our help is in the name of the Lord, who made heaven and earth" (Psalm 124:2, 3, 6, 8).*

God is a faithful God! He is still the same yesterday, today and forever. Amen! I belt it with you: if you can trust the Lord, even if people call you names, never mind; your expectation is on your way, no matter what you are going through right now. Say amen! (Please, read this: Psalms 46:1-5).

2. **Depend on the grace of God**—It is the grace of God that makes men great. Grace is defined as unmerited favor. But let me quickly say this: there is the power dimension and the favor dimension of the grace of God; but in this book, we shall be concentrating on the favor dimension of grace. If you want to know more about the power dimension of grace, please, get my book, **"EXPRESSING THE SUPERNATURAL".** You can get it from online stores like amazon.com or barnesandnobles.com.

In the kingdom of God, no one has ever amounted to anything in the energy of the flesh. See what the bible says about that: *"We have heard with our ear, O God, our fathers have told us what work thou didst in their days, in the times of old. How thou didst drive out the heathen with thy hand, and plantedst them; how thou didst afflict the people, and cast them out. For they got not the land in possession by their own sword, neither did their own arm save them: but thy right hand, and thine arm, and the light of thine countenance, because thou hadst a favor unto them" (Psalms 44:1-3).*

The arm of flesh (human strength) will always fail people. Only the grace of God is what sustains. The same God, who helped Israel to occupy where they are today, will help you achieve your dream also in Jesus' name!

By human calculation, as one born of a poor parent, I should not be where I am today. It took the grace of God for me to rise above all the negative odds that surrounded my life. If you came from such poor background, where no one was there to help out, you would know what I really mean. The bible says, *"So then it is not of him that willeth, nor of him that runneth, but of God that showeth mercy"* (Romans 9:16).

How can one have access to the grace of God?

1. Be born again
2. Be humble before God (James 4:6)
3. By prayer (Hebrews 4:16)
4. By locating God's plan and purpose for your life (Luke 4:18, 19; Romans 15:19)

Whatever God will do for any man, it is because such man is a heavenly means of achieving a divine purpose here on earth. For you to succeed in the pursuit of the assignment of God in your life, God will always give you His equivalent grace for accomplishment. God's purpose in your life is your major qualification for the grace of God. (Read my book on **"Fulfilling your destiny with ease"**). It will surely bless your life!

5. Possess the knowledge of God and of His Son, Jesus Christ (1 Peter 1:2)
6. Have faith in God in every situation (Romans 5:2)
7. Live a righteous life (Romans 5:21)
8. Follow the leading of God all the time

What the grace of God will do in your life

1. It will make things easy for you (Zachariah 4:6-10)
2. It will separate you from the common unto the uncommon (Esther 2:2, 8-23)
3. It will help you achieve the impossible. You do hear people say things like, "This can only be by God". That is a statement showing divine involvement in human affairs.

Nichodemus said to Jesus, *". . . for no man can do these miracles that thou doest, except God be with him" (John 3:2B).*

4. It will cause you to obtain favor or the assistance of people without struggling for it (Luke 8:1-3). King Solomon received a lot of material favors in his days, which helped him to achieve God's dream in his life—the building of the temple. I see you succeeding too in Jesus' name!

3. **Connect yourself to a prophetic anointing—**The bible says, *"Believe God, and ye shall be established; believe also his prophet, and ye shall prosper" (2 Corinthians 20:20).*

The prosperity of a nation is tied to the ministry of a prophet. The bible also said that *"By a prophet, the Lord brought Israel out of Egypt; and by a prophet was he preserved" (Hosea 12:13).*

Prophetic anointing will always bring people to the place of divine fulfillment. God has designed the prophetic ministry for the lifting and establishment of His people in success and prosperity. Your connection to this divine gift will determine your success in life. Any man without a prophetic covering is vulnerable to failure, demonic attacks, mishaps, and all manners of evil works.

The anointing incumbent on the prophetic office is like the two-edged sword. If it is provoked positively, it will release blessings of all kinds; but if it is provoked negatively, it will release negative spells that leads to failures, mishaps, physical disabilities, spiritual impediment, etc.

Let us look into these verses of the bible, *"Then, all the people of Judah took Uzziah, who was sixteen years old, and made him king in the room of his father, Amaziah. And he sought God in the days of Zachariah, who had understanding in the visions of God: and as long as he sought the Lord, God made him to prosper. And God helped him against the Philistines, and against the Arabians that dwell in Gurbaal, and the Mehunim. And the Amorites gave gifts to Uzziah: and his name spread abroad even to the entering in of Egypt; for he strengthened himself exceedingly" (2 Chronicles 26:1, 5, 7, 8).*

King Uzziah had the help of the Lord. What were his secrets?

1. He stayed under a prophet ministry.
2. He did that which was right in the sight of God, because he constantly received divine teachings from a prophet of God.

Again, the bible says, *"And he made in Jerusalem engines, invented by cunning men, to be on the tower and upon the bulwarks, to shoot arrows and great stones withal. And his name spread far abroad; for he was marvelously helped, till he was very strong"* (2 Chronicles 26:15). I see help coming your way from now in Jesus' name!

In the days of King Zerubbabel, he was building the house of God, when, suddenly, the work stopped. The enemies tried to hinder him, but as soon as prophet Haggai and Zachariah stepped in prophetically, the story changed for the better. The bible recorded that the work of God continued by the help of God through the prophesying of the prophets, until the work of God was completed. Prophetic ministry is one of the ways to gain access to divine help (Ezra 5:1, 2; 6:14).

I see God helping you too in Jesus' mighty name! As a Prophet of God, I declare that every work of your hands should receive divine speed and favor for accomplishment right now! I declare that you go forward from now! I command stagnation to be removed from your life right now! I command your enemies to be humiliated before you! I see you rising above all obstacles of life in your journey of success! Nothing will be able to stop you in the precious name of Jesus! Amen!

CHAPTER TWO

The vital ingredients for making success without sweat

Every good soup is made of correct ingredients. Without the correct ingredients for a particular soup, the soup will not give the expected taste. The same way, every good success is a product of correctly applied needed ingredients.

Note this: success is the achievement of God's plan and purpose for your life progressively without the lack of what is needed at every facet and dimension of your divine project.

Many great men and women of God in the bible days possessed these vital ingredients for success I am about to unfold to you. (They are divine virtues). Your success will be limited to human achievement, if you lack these important virtues of a successful life. I called them "The ingredients for success".

What are these ingredients?

1. The fear of God:

"Who, then, is the man that fears the Lord? He will instruct him in the way chosen for him. He will spend his days in prosperity, and his descendants will inherit the land" (Psalms 25:12, 13) (NIV).

"The secret of the Lord is with them that fear him; and he will show them his covenant" (Psalms 25:14) (NIV).

The fear of God indicates reverence for God and His word. It is a spiritual substance that is deposited in every child of God by the Holy Spirit. It is a divine inherent instinct that serves as an umbilical cord between us and God. Sometimes, it is called conscience by psychologists. God uses it to guide us in His way. It keeps us within the boundary of righteousness. It is the pivot around which our godly life revolves.

The bible said, if a man possesses this wonderful ingredient called the fear of God, he is bound to prosper in life. It also said that God will instruct such one in the way he should go in life in order to avoid wrong investment, wrong business partners. He does this by

15

making such one lose his inner peace over an adventure. Please, when this happens to you, make a 'U' turn immediately. Divine peace or lack of it is the function of divine approval. If God Okays your intention, you will be full of joy and inner tranquility; but if not, the opposite will be your experience. In other word, the fear of God controls our peace.

The bible said that the fear of God is the beginning of wisdom. And, know for sure that every great success is traceable to the act of wisdom. Wisdom leads you in the right path. You can hardly make any mistake in the right path.

"I, wisdom, dwell together with prudence; I possess knowledge and discretion. I walk in the way of righteousness, along the path of justice, bestowing wealth on those who love me and making their treasures full" (Proverbs 8:12, 20, 21) (NIV).

The King James Version says, *"I lead in the path of righteousness"*. This implies that divine wisdom only operates in the sphere of righteousness. if you lose righteousness, you will be disconnected from divine wisdom. They are interwoven.

"The fear of God is to hate evil" (Proverbs 8:13) (NIV). You can't fear God and still love sin. Sin dreads every man that fears God. And this is why God would want to help

such one to choose the way to go and to help him fulfill his divine mission on earth. Another way to fear God is to acknowledge Him in everything we do. If the peace of God does not abide with you in the way you chose to follow, don't continue. The end may be disastrous!

God is willing to lead you. The bible says, *"I will instruct you and teach you in the way you should go; I will counsel you with my loving eye on you" (Psalms 32:8 NIV).* It is impossible to fail when you follow the leadership of God keenly. The additional privilege of following divine leadership is that you will enjoy divine protection. It says, *"I will counsel you with my loving eye on you".* Amen! This promise shows that God is absolutely committed to the success of a child of God. Your success means so much to Him. Follow Him and be free from every other form of fear in life!

Success is part of your divine design. You are not design to fail in life. But you need to take cognizance of these ingredients I am unveiling to you, and put them to work, if you must be successful and fulfilled in life.

There was one man in the bible days that possessed this vital virtue, "The fear of God", and I will like to show him to you: *"There was a man in the land of UZ, whose name was Job; and that man was perfect and upright, and one that feared God, and eschewed evil . . . so that this man was the greatest of all the men of the east" (Job 1:1-3).*

It is possible to fear God and still be successful. In fact, the fear of God is in the root of a true success. The fear of God pays! You can't fear God and be small or fail in life.

In Psalms 25:14, where we read at the beginning of this sub-topic, the bible declared that the secret of the Lord is with them that fear him. The word 'Secret' means the key to the door of success in anything you may want to do. The man Job we just read about traded on the secrets of God. Let's read about him more; *"I long for the past, when God took care of me, and light from his lamp showed me the way through the dark. I was in the prime of life, God All-powerful was my closest friend, and all my children were nearby. My herds gave enough meek to bath my feet, and from my olive harvest flowed rivers of oil"* (Job 29:1-6).

This man, Job, was a man of honor, affluence and influence, and was a great congressman in his country. You can't possess the secrets of God and remain in the bottom of life. Remember Daniel (Daniel 5:11, 12).

If you read the account of Daniel in Daniel chapter one, you would see the clear evidence of the fear of God in the depth of the young man's heart. That was the reason behind the display of the kind of wisdom that resided in him that was given to him by God, which placed him above his equals in his days (Daniel 6:1-3).

I see you rising out of the obscurity of life in the name of Jesus! I see God's fear distinguishing you from the crowd this year, if you walk in it. You will never be hidden anymore! Confusion is bowing out of your life in haste! By the virtue of God's revelation to you, your situation is getting an answer and changing for the better speedily! You will never be the same again! Amen!

2. **Integrity:** What is integrity? Advanced Learned Dictionary definition says it is the quality of being honest and upright in character. It also says it is the state or condition of being complete.

To me, it is one of success' great pillars. Potentials attract attentions to an individual; but integrity sustains profitable relationship. Remember, it takes relationship to climb high on the ladder of success. No matter your potentials or talents, if people do not accept you, you will be unprofitable to them.

Dishonesty is a disease that gradually eats up the internal organs of success. The bible says, *"A good name is more desirable than great riches; to be esteemed is better than silver and gold" (Proverbs 22:1) (NIV)*. People cannot make any tangible commitment to you until they find you trustworthy enough. Honesty is what will project you and not your struggle for human connections. No matter your connection, if you are found to be dishonest, a fatter damage can be done to your most profitable relationship.

No man entrust a great responsibility into your hand without trusting you first. Doing so would be a risk. Trust is the bedrock for inter-personal success. If you can relate well, you are in for a great consistent success.

Let's see some a few examples from the bible on this subject: *"He chose David also his servant, and took him from the sheepfolds: from following the ewe great with young he brought him to feed Jacob his people, and Israel his inheritance. So he fed them according to the integrity of his heart . . ." (Psalms 78:70-72).*

King David was chosen by God because of the integrity of his heart. Even in great companies, nobody puts you in a sensitive position without proving your character to be trustworthy first. Lack of integrity has ruined the destinies of so many people that are supposed to be great in their society. Before you are given a public office in any developed country, your background will undergo checks for several days to ascertain your trustworthiness. Also, no credit company would approve you for a credit card if you are not credit worthy. Integrity is a very strong factor for the bond of unity. It is a weapon of war in the days of turbulence. Selah!

Another man that succeeded in his days was Joseph, the eleventh son of Jacob. He was a Hebrew boy, who became a Prime minister in a foreign land. His account in the bible shows that he was an epitome of honesty. His Egyptian master entrusted all his business empire to him because he found him honest and faithful, apart from the fact that he was successful by the hand of God.

What about the account of Abraham? God said concerning him, ". . . *shall I hide from Abraham that thing which I do; seeing that Abraham shall surely become a great and mighty nation and all nations of the earth shall surely be blessed in him. For I know him that he will command his children and his household after him, and they shall keep the way of the Lord, to do justice and judgment; that the Lord may bring upon Abraham that which he had spoken of him"* (Genesis 18:17-19).

It takes trust to speak of someone in this manner. It is a great privilege for God to entrust one with a very great mission like that of Abraham. The question is, "Can God trust you?" Abraham was tested by God in many ways before He could trust him.

What about Jotham? The bible says, *"Jotham remained faithful to the Lord his God and he became a very powerful king"* (2 Chronicles 27:6) (CEV). Isn't that great? It is to have integrity before God and man. No matter where you are today, your dream can see the light of the day by the virtue of integrity. Just walk before God and be perfect!

3. Meekness: *". . . God opposes the proud but gives grace to the humble" (James 4:6) (NIV).*

Who is a humble person? It is someone that respects the ordinances and commands of God; someone who is a true follower of the instructions of God; someone who acknowledges God in all his ways; one who respects authorities; one who realizes and accept his weaknesses and seeks ways of handling them; one who is able to say, "I am sorry", when he is wrong; one who does not claim to be all-knowing; one who does not esteem himself more highly than he ought to; or one that does not despise people in his heart.

I heard of people who fell from a very high position to a very low estate because of pride. For example, people like Satan (Ezekiel 28:14-17; Isaiah 14:12-19); Nebuchadnezzar (Daniel 4), etc.

Prophet Moses was successful in his leadership and ministry because he was very meek. *"(Now the man Moses was very meek above all the men which were upon the face of the earth)" (Numbers 12:3).* God will always help a meek man. *"The meek will he guide in judgment: and the meek will he teach his way . . ." (Psalms 25:9). "The Lord lifteth up the meek: he casteth the wicked down to the ground" (Psalms 147:6). "For the Lord taketh pleasure in his people: he will beautify the meek with salvation" (Psalms 149:4).*

Humility, another word for meekness, pays a great deal. *"Notwithstanding, Hezekiah humbled himself for the pride of his heart, both he and the inhabitants of Jerusalem, so that the wrath of the lord came not upon them in the days of Hezekiah. And Hezekiah had exceeding much riches and honour: And he made himself treasuries for silver and for gold . . . Moreover, he provided himself cities, and possessions of flocks and herds in abundance: For God had given him substance very much . . . And Hezekiah prospered in all his works" (2 Chronicles 32:26-30).* Please, take the time to read the account of King Menasseh and King Amon (2 Chronicles 33:9-16, 20-25). I am sure it will bless your life. I also suggest that you read the account of King Zedekiah (2 Chronicles 36:11-21).

"A man's pride shall bring him low: but honour shall uphold the humble in spirit" (Proverbs 29:23).

"Before distruction the heart of man is haughty, before honour is humility" (Proverbs 18:12).

You cannot be humble before God and lose place with His goodness in life. God's eyes are always upon the lowly in heart. Jesus said, *". . . For I am meek and lowly in heart . . ." (Matthew 11:29).* That was why God used him so much, and he succeeded in his earthly ministry. See what he said in Philippians 2:5-11.

If you can possess this wonderful factor called, 'Meekness', you will surely go places in life.

4. **Merciful heart:** Like I said before, divine success is impossible without God. One of the factors that motivates God to release His helping hand to us for prosperity is 'Having a merciful heart' towards the poor, the needy, the orphans, the widows, foreigners in your land, and the fatherless.

The bible says, *"Pure religion and undefiled before God and the father is this, To visit the fatherless and the widows in their affliction, and to keep himself unspotted from the world" (James 1:27).* The New International Version puts it this way, *". . . to look after orphans and widows in their distress . . ."*

In Matthew 5:7, the bible says, *"Blessed are the merciful, for they shall obtain mercy".* And then, in chapter 7 verse 12, it says, *"So in everything, do to others what you would have them do to you, for this sums up the Law and the Prophets" (NIV).*

What you sow is what you reap. This was the secret of Job: *"Because I delivered the poor that cried, and the fatherless, and him that had none to help him. The blessing of him that was ready to perish came upon me: and I cause the widows heart to sing for joy" (Job 29:12, 13).*

No wonder God made him the richest man in the east in his time! Look at what he said further: *"I was eye to the blind and feet to the lame. I was a father to the needy . . ." (Job 29:15, 16 NIV).* God will always lift up those that care to the place of prominence.

A good leadership is all about relevance. What are you to your generation? How much do you care? See what God's word says: *"Whoever shuts their ears to the cry of the poor will also cry out and not be answered" (Proverbs 21:13 NIV).*

Again, it says, *"Whoever is kind to the poor lends to the Lord, and he will reward them for what they have done" (Proverbs 19:17 NIV).*

To live by the mercies of God is to live like someone without a fault, yet full of fault and not minded. Being merciful is what provokes the mercies of God towards you. A merciful heart is a blessing from God. Ask for it!

What does God demands of us? Read this: *"Is it not to share your food with the hungry and to provide the poor wanderer with a shelter—when you see the naked to cloth him, and not to turn away from your own flesh and blood? Then your light will break forth like the dawn, and your healing will quickly appear; then, your righteousness will go before you, and the glory of the Lord will be your rear guard. Then you will call, and the Lord will answer; you will cry for help, and he will say: Here am I. And if you do away with the yoke of oppression, with the pointing of finger and malicious talk, and if you spend yourselves in behalf of the hungry and satisfy the needs of the oppressed, then your light will rise in the darkness, and your light will become like the noonday. The Lord will guide you always; he will satisfy your needs in a sun-scorched land and will strengthen your frame. You will be like a well-watered garden, like a spring, whose waters never fail.*

Then, you will find your joy in the Lord, and I will cause you to ride on the heights of the land . . ." (Isaiah 58:7-11, 14 NIV).

Succeeding by the wings of God is living by the instructions of God. You can't live by God's word and not ride high in life. Success awaits those that obey God. You are about to see the dawning of God's glory on your life as you begin and keep showing mercy to those in needs. What happened to Job (as regarding the blessings of God) is about to happen in your direction!

Don't give up doing good things to people! Hear the word of God: *"Let us not become weary in doing good, for at the proper time, we will reap a harvest if we do not give up"* (Galatians 6:9 NIV).

5. **Righteousness**—Righteousness means a whole lot to divine success. It means being in right standing with God. It means doing what the word of God says. It means doing the will of God. It means obeying God's voice every time He speaks to you. When the Jews say you are righteous, they mean that you are prosperous, physically healthy, and you are in right standing with God. So, when you walk in righteousness, you are threading on the path of prosperity, because righteousness and prosperity are interwoven. When a Jew is not prospering, it means that there is a sin hiding somewhere in the person's life.

Poverty is a curse, according to the Jewish belief. Also, to them, sin and curse are interwoven. Read Deuteronomy 28:15-68. Nothing reduces a man to nothing like sin. It is deceptive, demoralizing and destructive.

But the word of God says, *"And if they be bound in fetters, and be held in cords of affliction; then he showeth them their works, and their transgressions that they have exceeded. He openeth also their eyes to discipline, and commandeth that they return from iniquity" (Job 36:8-10). It also says, "If they obey and serve him, they shall spend their days in prosperity, and their years in pleasure" (Job 36:11).*

The word, 'Prosperity' is another word for success. God's intent for you is to prosper in all ways—marriage, business, your career, your job, your health, etc. You are therefore supposed to prosper in all you do.

You can't live in sin and not experience calamities (Proverbs 1:23-27, 29-33). To verse thirty-two of the scriptures quoted above, the Contemporary English Version puts it this way, *"Sin and self-satisfaction bring destruction and death to stupid fools".*

Again, Righteousness is to have a conscience void of offence towards God and man. It is a very strong foundation for success. The bible says, *"Righteousness exalteth a nation: but sin is a reproach to any people" (Proverbs 14:34).*

Failure in life begins from the point of disregard for God's word. The book of Isaiah says, *"How I wish that you had obeyed my commands! Your success and good fortune would then have overflowed like a flooding river" (Isaiah 48:18)*. This was what he said to the Israelites in a foreign land. Then, in verse nineteen, it says, *"Your nation would be blessed with more people than there are grains of sand along the seashore. And I would never have let your country be destroyed"*.

Righteousness is motivated by the fear of God; and the fear of the Lord is the beginning of wisdom, and wisdom is the backbone of success. Wisdom is the ability to know what to do at any given time.

There is real blessing in obeying the word of God. The word of God says, *"Do not let this book of the law depart from your mouth; meditate on it day and night, so that you may be careful to do everything written in it. Then, you will be prosperous and successful" (Joshua 1:8 NIV)*. King James Version says, *". . . for then thou shalt make thy way prosperous, and then thou shalt have good success"*.

To get things right is to do it God's way. And you are not going to be just successful, but your success will be a good one.

I see you succeeding in the name of Jesus! You will certainly fly high on the wings of God, as you follow divine instructions this year! Amen!

6. **Spiritual sensitivity to divine leading**—This talks about the hearing ear. Many have made shipwreck of the businesses, marriages, companies and institutions because of lack of sensitivity to the leading of the Holy Spirit, the custodian of good success.

The word, 'Sensitivity' here has to do with a divine knowing of 'What', 'When', and 'How' the Spirit of God wants you to go about a matter or a pursuit. It also has to do with being spiritually smart or alert to spiritual realms, or having a divine knowledge of unfolding or hidden matters that are detrimental or supportive to your success.

Our natural senses are prone to mistakes because humans are not all-knowing. We are limited as a result of the human body we are wearing. God knows we are capable of making serious mistakes that is why he sent us His Holy Spirit to guide us rightly in our daily activities. *"The Spirit shows what is true and will come and guide you into the full truth" (John 16:13 CEV).*

"But Christ blessed you with the Holy Spirit. Now the Spirit stays in you, and you don't need any teacher. The Spirit is truthful and teaches you everything. So stay one in your heart with Christ just as the Spirit has taught you to do" (1 John 2:27 CEV).

"But the counselor, the Holy Spirit, whom the Father will send in my name, will teach you all things . . ." (John 14:26 NIV)

When Jesus was on this earth, he knew when to make a move and what to do in any situation. Even when he was faced with the temptation from the Pharisees, Sadducees and Lawyers, by sensitivity, he overcame them all. He never spoke or took any action based on pressure of any kind. He was always listening to the Holy Spirit (John 5:30). This was why he was excellent in his earthly ministry. He came to teach us how to live a successful live here on earth. (Please, read the book of Saint John's Gospel).

So many people do things just because others are doing the same. Some do things just to please the masses. These kinds of attitudes have rendered many bankrupt, and led many into failure in leadership and marriage; and some have missed their destinies. One stupid step has the capacity to wreck your destiny, marriage, ministry, organization, company, or relationships, except God intervenes in your case. You need divine direction always! Read Acts 27.

Our intellect can put us into trouble, if we put all our trust in it and not in God. Human ideology can fail, but God's leading can never fail. Although, it may not suggest positively to our human sense but it will be justified at the end, if we follow His leading. Sometimes we allow our natural sense of judgment to overrule the inner voice of the Holy Spirit, which may eventually lead us into trouble.

There is one man I like to talk about, whenever I talk about divine leadership: the man called, 'King David'.

After the death of King Saul, by the Spirit of God, David was led to go to Judah. Being sensitive to divine leading, he went to Hebron, one of the cities of Judah. As soon as he got there, the people of Judah made him King, after which he became the king of Israel. If he were not sensitive to the leading of God, he might not become king in the first place, or maybe, his destiny would have been delayed (2 Samuel 2:1-4).

Many would have been successful and fulfilled today, had they hearkened to the nudging of the Holy Spirit in their hearts. God is willing to lead you, but are you willing to hearken to him?

God, speaking in his word, said, *"I will instruct thee and teach thee in the way which thou shalt go: I will guide thee with my eyes. Be ye not as the horse, or as the mule, which has no understanding . . ." (Psalms 32:8, 9).* Another scripture says, *"And thine ears shall hear a word behind thee, saying, This is the way, walk ye in it, when ye turn to the right hand, and when ye turn to the left" (Isaiah 30:21).*

The first scripture among the ones we have just read above makes us know that it is possible to hear God and not understand his voice. The gift of sensitivity delivers us from making fatter errors that are capable of rendering our lives unproductive or dormant.

How does God lead?

1. God leads us by an undeniable peace in our hearts. Any time you are losing your inner peace, check out your moves or decision. There could be an error that could possibly lead to trouble ahead of you that God is trying to keep you from.

Sometimes, the loss of peace in your heart could possibly mean that God is demanding your attention towards something he wants you to do that you are not aware of. Never ignore such feeling; it could deliver you from loses or bring you into unusual breakthrough in your life.

2. God leads us through a deep inner perception of things as in the case of David. But sometimes, we can perceive wrongly. The only thing that can justify our perception as being right is the peace of God in our spirit.

How to grow your sensitivity

1. Read the word of God always.
2. You can grow your sensitivity by engaging in prayer and fasting often.
3. You can also grow it by praying in the Holy Ghost (praying in tongues).

4. You can also build it by being willing to obey the leading of God at all cost; even if it means to offend people around you.

7. **Obedience to covenant demands**—God believes in covenant. It is the best way God relates with His Children. If you understand the covenant principles of God, nothing will be impossible to you. Everything God does is only within the boundary of His covenant and mercy. So, if you want to win God's backing in everything you do, you must know how to operate within those boundaries.

See what the bible says; *"Know therefore that the Lord thy God, he is God, the faithful God, which keepeth covenant and mercy with them that love him and keep his commandment to a thousand generation. Thou shalt therefore keep his commandment, and the statutes, and the judgment, which I command thee this day, to do them. And he will love thee, and bless thee, and multiply thee: he will also bless the fruit of thy womb, and the fruit of thy land, thy corn, and thy wine, and thine oil, the increase of thine kine, and the flock of thy sheep . . . Thou shalt be blessed above all people"* (Deuteronomy 7:9, 11, 13, 14).

What is covenant? It is an agreement, (flexible or rigid), between two or more people. It is also a constitution binding on the subjects of a kingdom. It contains 'Dos' with equivalent blessings, if obeyed; and 'Don'ts' with equivalent punishments, if violated. It is therefore the choice of the parties involved. But thanks be unto God, for he never breaks His covenants. The bible says, *"Nevertheless, my loving kindness will I not utterly take from him, nor suffer my faithfulness to fail. My covenant will I not break, nor alter the things that is gone out my lips" (Psalms 89:33, 34).*

God is the fulfiller of whatever He says. *"God is not a man that he should lie; neither the son of man that he should repent: hath he said and shall he not do it? Or hath he spoken and shall he not make it good" (Numbers 23:19)?* He said, *". . . for I am alert and active, watching over my word to perform it" (Jeremiah 1:12 AMP).*

From ages, man has been the one being unfaithful to the keeping of God's covenant. Like in every organization, from the day someone gets born again, he/she registers into the divine covenant of God over God's kingdom. God made this covenant with the Israelites, but Jesus Christ brought us into it via his death on the cross (Galatians 3:13, 14 NIV).

Paul, the apostle, illustrated how we (the gentile nations) were connected to these awesome blessings by the death of Christ with the analogy of the "Vine and its branches" in Romans 11:1-7, 11-19. I encourage you to read those verses for proper understanding.

The moment one joins the body of Christ by accepting Christ as his/her personal Lord and savior, he/she becomes bound to 'Abrahamic' covenant and blessings; and this covenant is a must to be fulfilled in such a person's life. It is the fulfillment of these covenants that brings about our lifting, security, all-round blessings, and fulfillment in life generally.

Nothing interests me like obeying the written or spoken words of God, and I have never seen my life going backward. God has been faithful to His word in my life; and I am so sure he will do the same to you, if you obey His word at all cost.

Meeting the terms of God's covenants is to commit God to do His part, and He will always remain faithful. *"To the faithful, God will show himself faithful . . . but to the devious, he will show himself shrewd" (2 Samuel 22:26, 27 NIV).* The covenant promises do not work for those that are unfaithful to the covenant demands (Micah 2:7B).

You have no right to make any claim on God's promises when you have not fulfilled your part of the covenant demands, whether it has to do with divine health, financial prosperity, protection, etc. Every of God's promise is tied to a condition(s); until you meet the condition(s), you are not entitled to its equivalent blessing(s). I mean, God will not respond to his part of the covenant, until you have fulfilled your part. Be a covenant practitioner and you will be in for a life full of God's blessings.

I will not be able to give you all the scriptures containing all the promises of God here, but let me reveal a few to you: *"This book of the Law shall not depart out of your mouth, but you shall meditate and do according to all that is written in it. For then you shall make your way prosperous, and then you shall deal wisely and have good success"* (Joshua 1:8 AMP).

This has to do with studying God's word, meditating on what you read until you believe it; and then, speaking out your conviction (giving a verbal expression to your conviction). It also has to do with fulfilling your part of the promise (covenant). When you do those things mentioned above, you commit God to confirm what you say. For the bible says, *"Say unto them, As truly as I live, Saith the Lord, as ye have spoken in mine ears, so will I do to you"* (Numbers 14:28).

Your present experience is a product of the response of God to your daily confessions. If you change what you say, you will definitely change what you experience. To live a positive life, you must align your mindset with God's word in order to constantly speak his word over any ugly situation that confronts your life on daily basis and provoke the divinity to bring to pass what they hear you say. This is how to live in the realm of miracles.

Understanding God's word and doing what it commands sets you on high. I see you rising to the place of affluence and prominence in Jesus' name!

8. **The 'God's presence' factor**—The presence of God with someone is a prove of divine approval for sonship. The bible says, *". . . Nevertheless, the Lord knoweth them that are his" (2 Timothy 2:19).* God's presence is an evidence of divine seal. God's presence is the reason for all the unusual positive happenings in your life—favor, honor, success, the help of men, unusual promotions, insurmountable victories over ugly circumstances, and great prosperity (Deuteronomy 2:7).

You cannot be led by God, if He is not with you. When he leads the way, you will definitely hear his voice; when you hear his voice and follow his leadership, you are bound to succeed in your pursuit. Sweatless success in anything you do as a child of God is traceable to the presence of God in your life. Jesus experienced this (Acts 10:38)!

The scriptures says, *"With men, it may be impossible but not with God; for with God, all things are possible (Mark 10:27).* This implies that if you completely rely on human expertise, you may not succeed in your adventure; but if you put your trust in God, while he is with you, nothing will stop you from prospering in your divinely inspired pursuit.

Prophet Moses said to the children of Israel, saying, *"The Lord your God has blessed you in all the works of your hands. He has watched over your journey through this vast desert. These forty years the Lord your God has been with you, and you have not lacked anything (Deuteronomy 2:7 NIV).*

In the days of Joshua, the successor of Prophet Moses, The ark of God was with them, from where God constantly spoke to them, giving them divine direction on every matter, including that of dividing of the River of Jordan (Joshua 3) and of the fall of the wall of Jericho (Joshua 6).

There is no situation that is bigger than your God. As far as God is with you, every seemingly insurmountable mountains is giving way for you right now in the name of Jesus Christ! Read Psalms 114:1-8 and see the account of the results of God's presence.

Let us understudy the story of Joseph: *"But the Lord was with Joseph, and he (though a slave) was a successful and prosperous man; and he was in the house of his master the Egyptian. And his master saw that the Lord was with him and that the Lord made all that he did to flourish and succeed in his hand. So Joseph pleased (Potiphar) and found favour in his sight . . . And (his master) made him supervisor over his house and he put all that he had in his charge. From the time that he made him supervisor . . . the Lord blessed the Egyptian's house for Joseph's sake; and the Lord's blessing was on all that he had in the house and in the field"* (Genesis 39:2-5).

You can't carry God's presence and be stranded in business, marriage or whatever you are doing in the name of the Lord. If what you are doing is based on God's leading, success is sure because the pursuit of God's purpose attracts the presence of God (God's backing); and his presence provides his instructions, and his instructions offers his wisdom, and his wisdom makes a success out of anyone.

When you are on course with God, he commands his blessings on whatever you do. I have never been stranded in my life, except when I am not on course with him.

If you must succeed in life, you must walk with the Lord and do what he likes daily. Jesus said, *"And he that sent me is with me: the father hath not left me alone; for I do always those things that please him" (John 8:29).* No wonder he was very successful in his earthly ministry. He also operated a kind of wisdom the world had never seen before his time because God tells him what to do in every situation (John 5:30; 8:28), and people wondered where his wisdom came from (Mark 6:2). That was interesting, right? The World has not seen anything yet; because your turn to show them the display of God's infinite wisdom has finally come!

Imagine Joseph (a slave youth) giving solution to a whole country's problem! It doesn't matter what your age, academic level, or social status is, it is the wisdom of

God in your life that counts. A wise man said, "When wisdom is in place, your age will be forgotten".

I see you celebrated on News papers, Press Release, Media, and on the internet world in Jesus' name!

What God likes

1. Righteousness (which includes liberality to the widows, fatherless and the needy (James 1:27)
2. Obedience to His leading
3. Commitment to His purpose and will
4. Seeking after His will in everything you do

The opposite of these things is what God hates.

The Holy Spirit is described as 'The angel of his presence' (Isaiah 63:9). He is the evidence and the embodiment of God's presence with us today. Listening to him, obeying him and following his leadings are what will determine your success here on earth.

I, therefore, commend you to the Holy Spirit, who is your comforter, counselor, helper and teacher (1 John 14:26). You shall be successful in life in Jesus' name!

9. **Travailing in prayer**—Prayer is an employable mechanism that makes things happen. The word 'Travail' is something that relates to the pain of

childbirth. It is not an easy pain, but it tends to vanish as soon as the baby is born.

Prayer is designed by God for the bringing forth of vision. When a vision is conceived and passes through the process of development and the bearer does not travail to give birth to it, he/she may eventually die with the vision; except God intervenes.

Our covenant Fathers (the Patriarchs) were men of exemplary prayer attitude. Abraham was a man of prayer (Genesis 13:3, 4); Isaac was a man of prayer (Genesis 25:21), Jacob, also, was a man of prayer (Genesis 28:18-22).

Prayer is the link of relationship between you and God. If this link breaks up, your relationship with God may be severed. And when this happens, failure becomes inevitable because, prayer is a way of communication between you and God, by which God relates the secrets of success to you. In any relationship, proper communication is the live-wire that sustains it. When there is a break in communication, there will certainly be a fracture, in any relationship.

To communicate means:

  a. to have a good relationship because of shared feelings and understanding (Colossians 1:7-11). Do you understand God's language?

b. to exchange information or ideas with someone (Numbers 14:11-22)

c. to minister something to someone, either in words or in kind.

A successful relationship between two individuals is a function of a good communication. If there is no living communication between you and God, your relationship with Him could be breached. I mean to say, if there is no interpersonal flow between you and divinity, you could become a living dead (Physically alive but spiritually dead), because if a man is not connecting heaven on daily basis, it will cause him to die slowly in the spirit, being that God is the source of the sustenance of the eternal life (Zoe) in any believer (Deuteronomy 8:3; Romans 1:17).

So, we can say that prayer serves as an umbilical cord between you and God. It also serves as a channel by which you are refilled with spiritual energy, helping you to continue to live by the life of God (Zoe).

Types of prayer

1. Individual prayer—this talks about one-on-one relationship with God. This type of prayer is the best, when it comes to making an enquiry from God to locate a divine direction concerning any issue; especially when stagnated, confused or

frustrated and know not what to do (Mark 1:35; Luke 22:41-44).

2. Collective prayer—this talks about a group of people coming together to lift up their voice to God in worship or for any other matter like needs, etc. If it is done in unity, it will have more force than that of individual type of prayer (Matthew 18:19; Acts 4:24-31, 33).

Note:

Prayer is a force in the hand of a believer, when approached systematically and scripturally. It is one of God's covenant tools for the realization of our glorious individual destinies in Christ.

Kinds of prayer and their application

Until you apply the formula for the kind of mathematical situation you are facing, answer to your calculation will be impossible, and all your efforts will be unprofitable. This is the same with prayer.

Nothing constitutes struggle like ignorance. People have mistaken noisy and tears-shedding people in the place of prayer for prayer warriors. Noise and tears are not prerequisites for receiving answer to your prayers. God can only be moved by your faith in His promises and covenant (Hebrews 11:6). The promises of God are divine contact points between you and God. If your prayers must be answered, you must connect with God through His promises. You can only believe God when you discover the substantial promises in His word (or call it, *"The evidences of things that you hope for*).

In this section, I want to treat the different formulas applicable to the different kinds of situation in order to help believers connect with God easily for speedy answers to their prayers each time they approach the throne of grace, and also to help them approach the throne of grace confidently, convincingly and boldly.

1. **Prayer of thanksgiving and praise**—this type of prayer is used mostly to access the gates and courts of the Almighty God easily (Psalms 100:2-4). It is also used to move God into action for your favor and to bring judgment upon your enemies (2 Chronicles 20:21-24; Exodus 15:11; Psalms 8:2). When other types of prayer fail, this one remains an undeniable force before God. King David knew this (Psalms 147:1)! It is a divine access code for signing in to a supernatural increase in life. (Psalms 65:5, 6; John 5:1-13). It is a divine invitation card for bringing down God's ultimate and irresistible presence, which is the backbone for expressing the supernatural (Psalms 22:3). Read my book, "EXPRESSING THE SUPERNATURAL". You can get it at amazon.com, barnesandnoble.com or trafford.com.

I encourage every believer to employ this type of prayer when they are in an unfavorable situation, instead of complaining or murmuring (1 Thessalonians 5:18). You can also use it to show appreciation to God for what He has done or promised to do.

2. **Prayer of request**—this refers to asking God for a need to be met (Matthew7:7). God is not obliged to do everything you ask of Him. Some of the things you are asking for could possibly be demanding your personal responsibility. This is why we should study the word of God to enlighten us to know our spiritual limitations so as to know where God can come in. God can only give attention to your request according to your limitations.

Babies can cry for every need and would be listened to, not an adult. An adult child cannot be asking his/her parent to help put on his/her cloths, when he/she is practically healthy. Such request could possibly engender anger instead of a positive response. Adults are taught how to handle things by themselves, but children can be assisted with any of their requests, if it is needed. This is one of the reasons why some prayers are not answered. Anything you can possibly do, God cannot do it for you. What He can only do for you is to help you discover what to do to enable you achieve your desired answers. So, be spiritually responsible!

3. **Prayer of command**—this is the kind of prayer that gives room for the expression of your divine authority. It allows the exercise of your spiritual muscles and dominion. Jesus taught us this (Mark 4:35-41; John 11:43-44)!

Everything God created has ears and they are at our command. This is justified by Prophet Micah and Jesus Christ (Micah 6:1; Mark 11:23). God, Himself, showed us examples from the beginning (Genesis 1:1-24).

The prayer of command is to speak things into existence, drawing strength from the spiritual (divine) realm by the help of visions through the ministry of the Holy Spirit. You can change the trend of things by engaging in this simple but profound act through the power of the Holy Spirit. God used the physically unseen things to produce the visible things. You too can, if you partner with the Holy Spirit in humility. Again, I say, read my book, "EXPRESSING THE SUPERNATURAL". It will throw more light on this subject.

You have the ability to decide what happens around you by the authority of God's word and will. Anyone given a political or leadership position is also given power and authority to function according to, and not below, the expectation of the authority over the jurisdiction where he/she rules. Therefore, know for sure that there is an expectation of you (as a god on earth) from heaven over your divine jurisdiction assigned to you, on behalf of heaven, on this earth (Psalms 82:6). So, it would be of your own interest to learn what it takes to put things under control here on earth in order to function maximally.

Prayer of command effects a change in situations. This is where believers should serve as solution bearers to this world, knowing that we are the salt of the world (Matthew 5:13; Mark 9:50), otherwise, we will lose our value of being a Christian.

Note:

God has laded us with unusual abilities in Christ to prove a difference in this world. Don't die in your situation, when you have the solution in your mouth. Use your mouth to chat the course of your life positively. Nothing may change until you start issuing command spiritually to your spiritual environment in order to see what you expect. Start commanding what you want and stop heralding your negative experiences. But remember, your success in this act of exercising your authority is completely dependent on knowing what the will of God is in all situations.

4. **Prayer of importunity (Persistency)**—Jesus showed us this in Luke 11:5-8 and Luke 18:1-8. No matter how unwilling God is, persistency will definitely put Him on the line of action to your advantage, when you pray rightly. Therefore, I

suggest that you do not give up easily, but pray until something happens (P.U.S.H), according to Dr. David Yonggi Cho of Yoido Full Gospel Church, South Korea. This is the basic reason why he established the Osanri prayer mountain in Kyonggi province, South Korea. Never give up easily! If you can persist, you will surely prevail! Evil may last for too long if you do not prevail over it in the place of prayer.

5. **Prayer of supplication**—this kind of prayer is done out of complete helplessness, humility and dependency on God, especially when you have exhausted all your strategies and skills in the pursuit of a particular goal or trying to solve a particular problem or when faced with a seemingly insurmountable challenge.

Most times, it is often done in tears. The Psalmist (King David) did it a whole lot (Psalms 123:1, 2); Hannah also did (1 Samuel 1:4-17); the children of Israel did it too (Exodus 2:23-25)! Nevertheless, know for sure that some cups (life's situations) are meant for you to drink unto your glorification in life, like in the case of Jesus (though he prayed earnestly for God to take the cup of death on the cross from him, but God did not listen to his cry, even at his greatest moment of his prayer time, where the sweat that came out of his body at that moment was described to be as thick as blood) (Proverbs 27:21). Remember, the pressure to pray this kind of prayer will mostly come when you are closer to your miracle.

I pray that God will hear your cry this month in Jesus' name!

6. **Prayer of intercession**—this is the kind of prayer that can be made on behalf of people, an individual, organizations, governments, or nations. Jesus did it for his disciples (John 17:1-26)! The early church did it for Apostle Peter, when he was imprisoned (Acts 12:5-19)! Elder James commanded the church everywhere to pray for one another (James 5:16). Even, Apostle Paul requested the brethren to pray for him (Hebrews 13:18; Ephesians 6:18-20).

7. **Prayer of inquiry**—this is a prayer mechanism that can be employed when you seem to be confused or frustrated in whatever you are doing or wherever you are in life generally. You can use it when you need a divine direction to know what to do or which way to go from where you are at a particular time of life. It serves as a divine compass for direction.

This is the kind of prayer that I don't joke with. It is my greatest source of strength for retaining focus in my ministry. It has really helped me to get to where I am today in life. If not for this kind of prayer, I would have completely loss the sense of purpose in life because, several times in my early days, as a minister of the gospel, I have lost direction due to several challenges that came my way. But thanks to God that I am where I am today!

It is unfortunate that many believers in the body of Christ do not know about this kind of prayer nor even subscribe to it. Rather than seeking God's face to hear him out for the way forward, when they are face with situations, many believers still try to reason it out with their limited natural senses, which often plunges them more into several mess worse than their formal state because, they followed the natural trends suggested by their natural senses and not the leading of the Holy Spirit.

The answer to this kind of prayer is always a way to victory, laughter and success. It is known as requesting for facts about a posing issue in order to get a breakthrough codes from heaven. You need a hyper-sensitive spirit, if you must gain maximum benefit in applying this kind of prayer, and you must have a constant developing understanding og the language of God. King David knew this (1 Samuel 23:1-5; 2 Samuel 2:1-4; 5:17-25)!

8. **Warfare prayer**—this kind suggests the use of spiritual weapons against the enemy. We have different kinds of weapon:

    1. The name of Jesus (Philippians 2:9-11)
    2. The blood of Jesus (Hebrews 12:24; Revelation 12:11).
    3. The word of God (Ephesians 6:10-12, 17-18)
    4. Speaking in unknown tongues (heavenly language) (Romans 8:26-27)

Only the divinely empowered radical Christians will experience a life of dominion and also live a victorious Christian life. Apostle Paul encourage Pastor Timothy to engage in spiritual warfare, if he must see the divine prophesies over his life come to pass in his lifetime (1 Timothy 1:18). The enemy is ready to wage war against your journey in life. The beast made war with the woman to stop her from being delivered of her baby boy (Revelation 12:1-5). Satan is still working tirelessly to see that belivers' dreams will be prevented or miscarried. Until you war with prophesies, they are, sometimes, not 'fulfillable'.

The enemy does not understand the language of tears. What he understands is outright confrontational combat. Until you learn to confront the kingdom of darkness by engaging them in a spiritual warfare, you may experience a long delay in fulfilling your dreams or divine assignment due to demonic resistance on your way to your glorification, breakthrough or break-forth out of obscurity (Luke 16:16). You need to wage war against the forces of hell (or you will compromise with them) in order to shine out in life. But compromising with the devil will keep you in perpetual slavery to Satan. Be courageous!

9. **Prayer of agreement**—the bible says that two are better than one, for they will have a better reward for their labor (Ecclesiastes 4:9-10). The prayer of

two or more persons (when done in oneness) is more productive than the prayer of an individual (Leviticus 26:7, 8). Even Jesus justified this fact (Matthew 18:19, 20)! This is where we talk about collective prayer.

The disadvantage of this kind of prayer (if done with someone untrustworthy) (Proverbs 11:13; 20:19) is that your secrets would have reached the ends of the earth before ever you get an answer from God, if at all it will reach heaven because it is not usually done in unison. Only do this kind of prayer with someone you trust!

Prayer formula

Prayer has a formula; and until you understand its formula, you will keep missing its results.

God is a personality; treat Him like one! Everyone likes appreciation, thanksgiving and acknowledgment. They serve as a soothing balm for the soul. They generate acceptance. They win the hearts of even your enemies. King David knew this (Psalms 100:2-4); Apostle Paul knew this (1 Thessalonians 5:18)! Jesus even taught us about this in his prayer formula (Luke 11:1-4)! Sincere acknowledgment and appreciation gives you entrance into heaven's gates and courts. This attitude is only an act of humility. Only the humble can appreciate people. Proud people never see the reasons to praise others.

There are some simple factors that will help you gain access to a successful prayer. I call them, "Prayer boosters". These factors are:

1. Heart of appreciation (Psalms 100:1-4)
2. Knowledge of God's will (Ephesians 5:17; Psalms 103:7)
3. Righteousness (John 9:31; Job 22:21, 26-28; 1 John 3:22)
4. Obedience to the voice of the Holy Spirit: where last you stopped obeying the voice of the Holy Spirit is where last you had a hitch-free relationship with Him, and that has put a breach between you and heaven without your knowledge. When this happens, eternal life (Zoe) would be breached and your prayer life will be dead. Also, you will not receive any revelation from God's word (Logos) when you read the bible. If you don't do anything about it as fast as possible, you will continue to struggle to honor God's word, and hearing God would also be shut away from you unless the voice of repentance.
5. Sensitivity to what God wants you to do every time in the place of prayer: don't just keep talking to God; learn also to listen to your inner man (your spirit). Prayer is a two-way thing. So, when you come to God in the place of prayer, be ready to relate with Him than talk, talk and talk. Most times, the answer to your prayers could come

through the still small voice of God that could possibly be missed or ignored.

I remember going to God in prayer for more than two weeks, asking God to tell me why people suffer; and God kept putting in my spirit a scripture from the book of Ephesians 1:18. I kept praying with it without knowing that my answer had already come. It took about six to seven months, when God revealed Himself to me in another direction, before I could understand that God was telling me the reason why people suffer from that scripture, but I was so insensitive to the voice of God. And, believe me, that scripture is what formed the foundation of my ministry today. Glory be to God for His patience with humanity!

6. A maintained relationship with the Godhead through the person of the Holy Spirit: the intensity of your relationship with God determines the level of success your prayer life would be.

Some people only relate with God when they have any problem. So, before they would be able to break the ice of silence between them and God, it will begin to prove prayer a hard thing to do. God believes in relating with you per second. He needs you around him every minute to show Him love through worship and praise from the bottom of heart. He wants you to always talk to Him. He loves your voice and the odor of your presence. He yawns for it all time. God misses you and needs your constant relationship!

Just think about the relationship between you and your earthly father. You can't have confidence enough to come and ask your father for anything except you are always with him, and there is no doubt of personality between you and him. That is exactly the same with God. The one who is always around him gets a speedy reply from him more easily than that person who comes and goes. Selah!

7. Love for God and humanity: lack of love, especially for the brethren, can breach eternal life from flowing in you. You die spiritually when you don't love, and God cannot relate with a spiritually dead Christian (1 John 3:14-15). If God would ever hear you and answer you, you must learn to love.

I love what the bible says here: *"And whatsoever we ask, we receive of him, because we keep his commandments, and do those things that are pleasing in his sight. And this is his commandment, that we should believe on the name of his Son Jesus Christ, and love one another, as he gave us commandment"* (1 John 3:22, 23). Your prayer from today should be, "God baptize me afresh with the spirit of love for you and the brethren". This is a wonderful request that bags an express answer from God. And again, it says, *"Is it not to share your food with the hungry and to provide the poor wanderer with shelter—when you see the naked, to clothe him, and not to turn away from your own flesh and blood? Then you will call, and the Lord will answer; you will cry for help, and he will say: Here am I" (Isaiah 58:7, 9 N.I.V).* It also went on to say, *"If a man shuts his ears to the cry of the poor, he too will cry out and not be answered" (Proverbs 21:13 N.I.V).*

Love is the greatest force for spiritual success! Even the Buddhists know this; although, they still find it very difficult to walk in love because true love is divine!

8. Fasting: this is not an act of starving oneself. A genuine fast is born out of a burden for an answer(s). When such burden comes, you tend to lose appetite for anything whatsoever. It happened to King David (2 Samuel 12:1-23)! A desperate hunger for God can also put you in such condition. Sometimes, all you can do is just drinking water or taking light meals just to sustain the body and to have strength (Psalms 63:1).

Fasting shows a genuine desire. God responds to the hungry and those that really thirst after Him (Matthew 5:6). Fasting is a great booster to receiving answer to your prayers if you pray in line with the will of God for you. It increases your spiritual sensitivity for perceiving the move of God and for discerning satanic activities.

9. Speaking in unknown tongues (heavenly languages) is another force for a successful prayer. Sometimes, you lack what to say in your common language, or even are speechless over some matters. It is even possible to pray an unnecessary prayer at certain times. This is why the help of the Holy Spirit is very essential to a Christian at such seasons. He knows you better, and he knows your situation better (Romans 8:26, 27). So he gives you a prayer language at such seasons of helplessness or produces spiritual groanings in your spirit (by praying for you) that cannot be vocally expressed.

Heavenly tongues also helps in building your faith in a mysterious way (Jude 20), and faith is an essential factor in the ministry of prayer (Hebrews 11:6).

10. The last I will mention here is vow (Job 22:27): remember Hannah's prayer (1 Samuel 1:9-20)! Also, remember Jacob's prayer (Genesis 28:10-22)!

Prayer without utterance

1. Obedience to God's word (Job 36:11; Deuteronomy 28:1-14): obeying God's word compels Him to fulfill His part of the covenant. God is too faithful to fail!

2. Liberality (Matthew 7:12; Luke 6:38; Proverbs 11:25)
3. Kingdom addiction (Matthew 6:33)
4. Positive imaginations (Ephesians 3:20)

Hindrances to prayer

1. Living an ungodly lifestyle (John 9:31)
2. Unbelief (James 1:5-8)
3. Ingratitude towards God
4. Proud heart (Luke 18:9-14)
5. Unforgiving attitude (Mark 11:24)

You have to shift your boat away from the above-mentioned prayer insulators if you need express answers to your prayers from God!

CHAPTER THREE

Profiting through the Prophets

Who is a Prophet? A Prophet is God's messenger. A Prophet is one that hears from God concerning divine directions. He is an agent of deliverance and prosperity. He is known as God's carpenter; an agent of divine change, preservation, divine restoration and a catalyst for divine speed in achieving success (1 Samuel 8:7-10; Zachariah 1:17-21; 2 Kings 6:24-7:1-19; Zachariah 4:4-9; Exodus 2:23-25; 3:7-10; Luke 5:1-7; 2 Chronicles 20:20; Ezra 5:1, 2; 6:14-15; 2 Chronicles 26:1-14).

Prosperity in God's kingdom here on earth is tied to the ministry of the Prophet (The prophetic office). To neglect the prophetic office is to sign up for a life of struggle. A turn-around miracle in God's kingdom is always the resultant effect of the prophetic anointing. Everyone needs a prophetic word in his/her life from season to season in order to advance from level to level, and from glory to glory.

The effect of the prophetic anointing on one's life is the evidence of God's stretched-forth arm to his/her favor. When you have done all you could and have prayed all you could over a particular situation facing you and nothing happens, locate a prophetic anointing. A prophetic anointing has the ability to bring someone out of obscurity.

Prophetic office was instituted by God as a channel of divine help. Where I am today is by the ministry of prophetic helping-hands I have encountered from time to time.

Examples of those that profited through the prophets

1. The Zarephath woman: this woman and her child was close to their grave by virtue of the economic crisis that broke loose by the word of Prophet Elija (1 Kings 17:1).

After she had a divinely arranged encounter with God's servant, Prophet Elija, for which she responded to his prophetic instruction, there was a reversal of the power of death that was against her household. God caused a turn-around to happen in her life by virtue of divine providence (Heaven' supply of flour and oil).

Divine instructions are heavenly designed gate-ways to a turn-around experience or breakthrough moments in life. If you can respond to God's instruction, your life will know no struggle.

The story of the Zarephath woman is always surprising to me because naturally, Prophet Elija seemed to be selfish in his request from the poor woman. Somebody said, "I only have the last meal for me and my son to eat before we die", and the seemingly mad Prophet (according to human ideology) said, "Bring for me first, and then anything remaining can serve for you and your son". Doesn't that sound crazy, uncompassionate and selfish? Of course, to human suggestion, it does. But Thanks to God that this woman was able to hear the voice of God behind the Prophet's word. The ability to discern God's voice in a prophetic instruction and be able to obey it is the grace that we all should pray for, if we must not miss any divine opportunity to experience God's power in our various situations. Sensitivity and obedience to divine instructions are keys to overcoming frustration, confusion, loss and stagnation in life. This is why we need to grow in the spirit and be spiritually conscious at all times to be able to catch divine signals—the direct voice of God or God's word through His prophets.

2. The Shunammite woman: this woman through her liberality towards the Prophet, Elisha, commanded the attention of God towards her seemingly impossible situation called 'Bareness'. Read the full story in 2 Kings 4:8-37.

According to the bible, Prophet Elisha did not introduce himself to her but she was sensitive enough to discover the anointing (2 Kings 4:9); she then made room for him in her duplex. That was an 'extra-mile' principle, and this single principle of liberality towards God's servant provoked an unexpected miracle of a baby boy for a baren aged woman. You need this kind of 'giving grace' in order to connect divine intervention in your situation today! I tell you the truth: if you can be sensitive enough to respond to the nudgings of the Holy Spirit, such kind of miracle would be your testimony.

3. A wife of one of the Prophets during B.C: her own case was that of debt incurred by her husband, who was working under the ministry of Prophet Elisha. It was that bad that the creditor demanded for her two sons to be slaves as a payment of the debt.

When she cried unto Elisha, a divine instruction was issued unto her by the Prophet, and her obedience made way for her victory over the wicked claws of debt. Read the full story in 2 Kings 4:1-7.

Are you experiencing any misery? Locate a genuine Prophet for a turn-around miracle. It is possible only by a little faith in the anointing upon a genuine Servant of God!

4. King Jehoshaphat and the people of Israel: this king was under duress by virtue of the armies of three combined nations (with a stronger military might) that besieged the nation of Israel to wipe her out of the world map. It was a challenging moment to King Jehoshaphat! How did he overcome? I believe that he had already been defeated in his mind, if not for the divine word that came to the people of Israel in a moment.

The funniest thing was that the prophecy that came did not conform to human ideology or reasoning. How can one nation (with less military might) engage in battle with three nations (with a stronger military might) and start singing and clapping of hands in the face of danger? Isn't that suicidal? But thank God for the people that understand the move of God!

The end-point of the scenario was mind-blowing. The three nations fought against themselves until no one was alive, while God's people (the Israelites) were praising

Harrison I. Enudi

God with songs and musical instruments. After the incidence, all that the children of Israel did was to gather treasures of gold, silver, etc. (2 Chronicles 20:1-30). I see your present challenge bringing your desired blessing to you at the end! You will overcome!

Somebody is about to have a romance with an unusual encounter for an unprecedented breakthrough or a turn-around in his/her ugly situation! Just locate the ministry of a prophetic anointing, and that would be it! It does not matter how long the challenge you are facing right now has been; one encounter with a prophetic anointing will show you the other side of life. You shall experience the season of laughter like that of Sarah, the wife of Abraham! "And Sarah said, God hath made me to laugh, so that all that hear will laugh with me" (Genesis 21:6).

5. King Uzziah: this was one out of many kings that experienced divine success in his little season of reign and had an unusual favor of the enemies of Israel, just because he had an uncommon mentor, Prophet Zechariah. The bible revealed that God made him to prosper and he was marvelously helped by God until he became very strong and his fame went beyond Israel as a great king. Read his account in 2 Chronicles 26:1-15.

Prophetic mentors are divine bridges to a great tomorrow (Proverbs 15:22).

6. The Israelites under captivity in Assyria: they were building the temple of God under King Cyrus, but the work came to a stand-still by virtue of some enemies and lack of building materials. Nevertheless, when the Prophets, Haggai and Zechariah, prophesied over the works of their hands (the building project), the hand of God moved on King Darius. Immediately, provision of building materials and political support took effect and the project prospered until it came to completion (Zechariah 4:6-9; Ezra 6:1-14; 5:1, 2).

God is still at work in our days! May you receive a prophetic helping-hand today in Jesus' name! You will prosper! Your situation is about to change for good by a divine help! Just locate a prophetic anointing!

God did not make a mistake in placing a prophetic office in the body of Christ; but it is your responsibility to draw from the grace of God incumbent upon the prophetic office in order to provoke a change in a positive direction. Any time there is an unproductive situation in your life, engage in prophetic obligation. It is a divine key for the miraculous.

7. Lot: he was under the 'Abrahamic' anointing in the days of Abraham (Genesis 13:2, 5-6). Staying under an anointed Prophet, who is operating under an open heaven can turn you into a financial baron.

Being righteous does not automatically qualify you for prosperity in the kingdom of God. The application of the understood principles of prosperity does. I shall talk more of this in the next chapter.

God repays wrong attitudes towards His Prophets

It is possible to despise a servant of God when you are not sensitive enough to observe him/her; and this has brought many people under a curse without their knowledge. The woman of Samaria almost fell into this trap (John 4:1-10).

Lack of the ability to discern spiritual men and women of God is a great danger! Ignorance is never an excuse to law. We need to grow in spiritual sensitivity.

Abraham saw the three men passing, and he was able to know that these men were not ordinary. He ran and bowed himself to them; afterward, he did a prophetic obligation to them. This was what broke the silence or seemingly delay of the prophecy over him concerning the birth of the heir (Isaac).

To be able to change the ugly tides of situations around you for good, you need to be able to discern the prophetic gifts God sends your way seasonally. They come from time to time to effect changes, but lack of recognition make people to lose the blessings that would have projected them unto the next level of their lives. And most times, instead of the anointing lifting us, we provoke the negative side of it against ourselves because of ignorance.

There are two sides to the prophetic coin. Every Prophet carries two sided anointing. They are born for the rising and falling of many (Luke 2:21-34). You can subscribe to either side of a prophetic anointing by your behavior towards a Prophet, knowingly or unknowingly.

The deliverance of Lot (Abraham's nephew) from not being destroyed along with Sodom and Gomorrah was because he was able to recognize the agents of heaven that came for the mission and gave them shelter, descerning that they were strange beings.

May the Lord help us by his Holy Spirit to be able to discern those that are sent for our good from time to time in Jesus' name!

Examples of those that suffered from the prophetic negative side

1. The family and generation of King Ahab (2 kings 9, 10): they suffered because their parent persecuted Prophet Elija for judging against their evil doings. You can see that even Kings could not stop the miseries that befell them from the Lord for tempering with the anointing negatively.

2. The sons of Eli: they were sexually abusing the women that came to offer sacrifices to God (a usurp of authority), and also made sleight of the sacrifices of God against their father's instructions (1 Samuel 2:12-17, 22-25, 30; 4:1-22). Because of these evil, their linage lose their priesthood forever after the two men's untimely death.

3. Koran, Dathan and Abiram: they measured themselves with Prophet Moses, and they and their generations were destroyed because of pride and arrogance against God's servant (Numbers 16:8, 9-15, 19-20, 24-33, 35).

4. The ten spies and their generations: they made sleight of the prophecy of God's servant, Moses, and never made it to the promise land (Numbers 14:22-38).

5. The forty-two youths that mocked Prophet Elisha were destroyed by bears as soon as he cursed them (2 Kings 2:19-24).

6. King Saul, who despised the instructions of Prophet Samuel, lost his kingly anointing and never ended well (1 Samuel 13:12-14).

7. Ham, the last son of Noah: he exposed his father's nakedness by way of despise and bagged his father's curse to be a servant to his brothers forever. This, today, has brought the black race and some part of

Asia and Arab to be under the rule of other continents. Trace the history for yourself and see what despise of the anointing (because of familiarity) can cause. But thank God for the blood of Jesus that brought the believers under the blessing of Abraham, which has saved us from the venom of the curse of Noah (Galatians 3:13, 14).

May God help us all! We will not suffer in Jesus' name!

Check out all the pages of the bible and you will discover that there is no one that offended the anointing that was free from God's wrath! Beware and be wise!

CHAPTER FOUR

Trading secrets for financial prosperity in God's kingdom on earth

P rosperity begins with the mind (3 John 2). The understanding of finance determines your financial height in life. No matter how educated you are or how spiritual you are, the knowledge of money (what brings it, how to grow it, how to sustain it, and how it moves) is needed; and it has no substitute.

I over-heard a prominent man of God once over the internet saying that your ability to manage money well determines your spiritual positioning in the God's kingdom. Remember the story of the talents! Money makes you valuable; without it, you cannot really matter to your society. Spiritual dominion without financial freedom results in spiritual catastrophe. Even if you are a servant of God, financial dominion is a great boost to your spiritual authority. It commands the honor of people. Abraham was a prophet but he was also respected as a prince because of his wealth (Genesis23:3-6). Isaac was also a prophet but the King of Philistines visited him because of his commanding wealth (Genesis 26:12-14, 26-29). The ministries of many anointed servants of God have been ruined because of lack of money. No matter how righteous you are, it is possible to walk in unrighteousness when you don't have money.

Success commands honor; and wealth is a great proof of success in the eyes of the people. Although wealth is not a good factor for measuring success, it reveals you to your world and attracts a global attention towards you. You cannot be wealthy and be hidden. You matter most to people based on your wealth. People may not like you but they cannot do without you when they need money or financial counsel.

Kingdom Prosperity

Kingdom prosperity is a divine order as the bible says, *". . . let the Lord be magnified, which hath pleasure in the prosperity of his servant" (Psalms 35:27)*. So, it is not a sin to be rich. God has durable riches made available to his children. He has never called anyone into poverty. Christ brought us into wealth by being poor for our sake (2 Corinthians 8:9). Moreso, he died to receive power, riches wisdom, strength, honour, glory and blessing for you and I (Revelations 5:12). This is why the bible says that we have been blessed with all spiritual blessings in the heavenly places (Ephesians 1:3), and we are complete in him (Colossians 2:10). He has given to us all things that pertain to life and godliness, but they can only be accessible by the knowledge of God and of Jesus Christ (2 Peter 1:3).

If you take time out to study the life of Abraham, you will discover that he was so blessed that no one that came out of his loins was identified with poverty as they walked in the covenant that Abraham walked in. That is the kind of blessing that God has brought us into through the death of Jesus Christ (Galatians 3:13, 14). God said, *"Look unto Abraham your father . . . for I called him alone, and blessed him, and increased him" (Isaiah 51:2).* The blessing of the Lord makes rich and he added no sorrow with it (Proverbs 10:22).

So, if you are poor in life, as a Christian, the revelation of the divinity could be lacking. If you can discover God and the mysteries of His word (Jesus Christ), you will certainly gain the understanding of the Kingdom you belong—your kingdom rights and the kingdom principles that can give you access to your rights.

You are too blessed to complain. I cannot be connected to the blessing of Abraham and be poor in life. Poverty is gone forever in my life. I have everything that pertains to life and Godliness. If Ishmael, the first son of Abraham, that was not even the heir, could not be poor but became a great nation (Genesis 21:13; 17:20), it is a complete evidence that I can never be poor!

As far as you are the seed of Abraham, whether by natural birth or by adoption, through the blood of Jesus Christ, you are not permeated to be poor because the covenant of blessing is upon you, except you are not walking in the covenant. But remember, the covenant of blessing demands your total obedience to God's word and the voice of the ultimate Ambassador of God's kingdom here on earth (The Holy Spirit)!

I repeat: the covenant of blessing only thrives on the platform of obedience, and it is possible to be walking in disobedience because of lack of the knowledge of God's word. Your greatest responsibility therefore is to strive to know God and His Son, Jesus Christ, by His word, if you must live in obedience, in order to gain access to your kingdom rights. You will never be poor in your life!

The secrets of kingdom prosperity

Physical factors:

1. **Work:** you could still be a child of God and still remain poor if you are doing nothing. The covenant of prosperity demands that you must be a worker, either as an entrepreneur or skillful personnel in the area of your divine endowment (talent, gifts or ability). Money comes majorly through taking advantage of people's ignorance and needs. Solving human problems, which is, doing for people what they cannot do for themselves and what they have no time to do for themselves are channels of making money. So, rise up and take advantage of these channels. Remember, God will only bless the works of your hands (Deuteronomy 16:15; 28:12). The blessing of Abraham will only find expression through the work of your hands.

I define work as an expression of personal ability and passion in order to meet a certain human need. Abraham was a farmer and a merchant in gold and silver (Genesis 13:2), and that was what his passion drove him for all the days of his life.

Nothing brings out the best out of you like doing what you are born to do. So, discover your calling! Read my book, "FULFILLING YOUR DESTINY WITH

EASE". Financial prosperity without inner satisfaction or fulfillment is living in misery. True prosperity is completely connected to your ability and passion; and it is also interwoven with pleasure and long life because of the joy that can be derived from minding your passion and making a living by what you could call your hobby.

Today, the nations that are involved in leveraging the ingenuity of people, skill development and marketing of what they produce are the richest in the world. There is nobody that is not laded with divine ability at creation. The trading of your ability in connection with your passion will definitely reflect in your value and your country's value.

Therefore, the number one factor for setting the law of kingdom prosperity in motion is working to service the need of your generation with your ability. Ability does not connote the expression of muscles but of talent or gift. You could be an engineer, a singer, a music or movie producer, a music instrumentalist, a doctor or nurse, a receptionist, a merchant, a designer, an artist, an actor or actress, a writer or a publisher, an industrialist or a manufacturer, a politician, etc., if you are diligent in your career, you will surely be celebrated, and you will prosper (Proverbs 22:29).

2. **Proper time management:** everybody is given equal time per day on earth. It is how you invest your time

that would prove if it will pay off in the future for you or not. You cannot bring back yesterday. Once time is past, it is past forever. Selah!

Note: a foolish labor is equal to time wastage. To invest your time into temporal pleasure (partying, clubbing, unfruitful conversation, uncertain ambition or pursuit, etc.) is to gravitate to becoming an indigent person in life. Read the following scriptures: Proverbs 10:4; 13:20; 12:11; 12:27.

A foolish labor simply means pursuing ambitions that cannot give you a deep sense of happiness, satisfaction or fulfillment at the end of your journey in life (when you are old), though you could be very rich.

Factors for managing one's time

a. discipline
b. vision of the future (the power to seize one's tomorrow)
c. a passionate desire to make a generational impact
d. diligence

All the above mentioned factors will govern your senses unto pursuing godly and fruitful relationship and engaging in things that will help you achieve your dream.

Note: Uncommon positive habits culminate in an uncommon lifestyle that will attract uncommon people in your life. Uncommon people in your life will result to having uncommon relationships that will constantly produce uncommon ideas. Uncommon ideas lead to uncommon activities that will eventually bring about uncommon success, which will again command more uncommon people into your life. This is why success begets success. It is called **'Success Cycle'**. The same principle applies to failure, when followed in the opposite direction.

3. **Proper money management:** money makes life beautiful. It has the capacity to transmute your dream into reality and to reveal you to your world. Lack of money can possibly limit your capacity to deliver your abilities to your generation, except you go by the principle of leverage. Without money, dreams can go into oblivion or obscurity. Many great dreamers have died with their dreams in the womb of their spirit because money, or the ideas to get it, was lacking. Also, improper money management can lead to bankruptcy or penury; but if well managed, can multiply.

Understanding money management

Managing money does not necessarily mean hording money or being unnecessarily frugal. How do we manage money?

a. Have an investment mentality. Think of growing your money. This will help you to prioritize your income properly and also save for the future, while building your assets. Also, you have to understand that the difference between the poor, middle class, and the wealthy is financial education—the knowledge of the difference between asset and liability, and financial discipline (spending based on needs and saving for investment purposes).

b. Think of real estate, leveraging profitable ideas, stock market, bonds, and personal goals and vision.

Spiritual factors

1. **Obedience to God's specific instructions:** one of the reasons for failure in human endeavors is ambition provoked by selfish interest.

In the kingdom of God, ambition is a wrong button to press when pursuing kingdom financial success. It is usually against the divine plan of God for one's life. Ambition is mostly governed by ego and it is also characterized with 'trial-and-error' method of doing things. One most times lack confidence in pursuing ambitious ideas, but you command divine confidence when pursuing real passion and positive mental pictures that is generated by the insight you gain into the possibility of a successful end when dealing with a divine goal.

When you are in partnership with divinity in the pursuit of any divine goal, the help of God is sure. God's help involves receiving divine wisdom, favor, courage, victories over all sorts of opposition, and the power to focus. Therefore, it is expedient for one to have a divine approval for one's pursuit before embarking on it.

Many people take loans (good debt) from financial institutions for business and go bankrupt in less than one or two years because divine purpose is not the base of such moves. Ambition is prone to frustration but divine pursuit is connected to divine backing.

Remember the story of Isaac in Genesis 26:1-14! In his days, there was a severe global recession that took place (Far worse than that of the days of his father, Abraham). He had an intention to migrate to Egypt (a centre of civilization and economic boom at that time); but God visited him in a dream and showed him what to do in the land of the Philistines, where he was living at that time. The verses of the bible quoted above detailed that he obeyed the instructions of God and made his way to becoming a financial baron in a nation where money tend to lose its ground. It is still possible in our time.

Nothing can establish your financial dominion like being obedient to God—the anchor of unending financial freedom. No matter your condition now, if you can follow what God wants you to pursue with your life, you would be on your way to victory over financial struggle forever. Peter knew this (Luke 5:1-7)! Abraham knew it too (Genesis 12:1-4; 13:1, 2)!

Obedience to God is a covenant obligation that must be given a proper attention to, if kingdom prosperity must reflect in one's life. See these scriptures: *"If they listen and obey God, they will be blessed with prosperity throughout their lives. All their years will be pleasant"* *(Job 36:11 NLT).* Another portion says, *"If you fully obey the Lord your God and carefully follow all his commands . . . the Lord will set you high above all the nations on earth. The Lord will grant you abundant prosperity . . ."* *(Deuteronomy 28:1, 2 NIV).* Another one says, *"Poverty and shame come to him who refuses instruction and correction, but he who heeds reproof is honored"* *(Proverbs 13:18 AMP).*

God is willing to lead you into financial success; but are you willing to follow (Psalms 32:8, 9)? Read these scripture: *"Oh that you had hearkened to my commandments! Then your peace and prosperity would have been like a flowing river . . ."* *(Isaiah 48:18 AMP).* Doing what God wants you to do, and doing it the way he wants you to do it will always guarantee your success.

2. **Living by God's word:** the word of God is divinely designed to program us into an unending parade of success in all areas of life. When we meditate on the word of God, it has the capacity to illuminate our

hearts with divine ideas or insight that can possibly open us up to great endeavors.

To live by God's word means to allow it lead our ways by programming our steps and governing our lifestyles.

What are the benefits of living by God's word? The bible says, *"Praise ye the Lord. Blessed is the man that feareth the Lord, that delighteth greatly in his commandments. Wealth and riches shall be in his house . . ." (Psalms 112:1, 3).*

Read this figurative story:

"Behold, the Assyrian was cedar in Lebanon with fair branches, and with a shadowing shroud, and of an high structure; and his top was among the thick boughs. The waters made him great, the deep set him up on high with rivers running round about his plants, and sent her little rivers unto all the trees of the field. Therefore, his height was exalted above all the trees of the field, and his boughs were multiplied, and his branches became long because of the multitude of waters, when he shot forth. All the fowls of the heaven made their nest in his boughs, and under his branches did all the beast of the field bring forth their young, and under his shadow dwelt all great nations. Thus was he fair in his greatness, in the length of his branches; for his root was by great waters. The cedars in the garden of God could not hide him: the fir trees were not like his boughs, and the chestnut trees were not like his branches; nor any tree in the garden of God was like unto him in his beauty. I have made him fair by the multitude of his branches: so that all the trees of Eden, that were in the garden of God envied him." (Ezekiel 31:3-9)

This story is like a man described in Psalms 1:1-3, who is living by God's word. He is like a tree planted by the rivers, whose leaves withers not, nor does it fail in bringing forth fruits in its seasons. You cannot put the root of your life by great waters (the word of God) and not become the envy of your generation. It happened to Isaac, when he obeyed the word of God by staying and farming in the land of the Philistines in the days of famine (Genesis 26:1-3, 12-14). I pray that you too will become the envy of your generation in Jesus' name! You will not be hidden in this world! The brightness of your greatness will be seen by your generation just like that of the Cedar of Lebanon! Your destiny will be incomparable with that of your peers!

To live by God's word is to live by divine wisdom; and divine wisdom is also the highway to divine prosperity. *"I wisdom dwell with prudence, and find out knowledge of witty inventions. Riches and honour are with me; yea, durable riches and righteousness." (Proverbs 8:12, 18).*

Divine wisdom is the mother of creativity. Invention and innovation are impossible without divine wisdom. We all need divine wisdom on daily basis.

3. **Liberality:** this is a universal law that has effect, both in the hands of the godly and the ungodly (Ephesians 6:8). No matter the effort of humans to become rich, there will still be the poor and needy in the world. A part of the covenant blessings God has for us is packaged in the poor and the needy. But this blessing is dormant and ineffective until it is provoked by generosity and liberality. This is why only the liberal can access the uncommon and enriching blessings.

Read these scriptures: *"He who gives to the poor will not want, but he who hides his eyes (from their want) will have many a curse" (Proverbs 28:27 AMP). "Giving to the poor will keep you from poverty, but if you close your eyes to their needs, everyone will curse you" (Proverbs 28:27 CEV). "He who despises his neighbor sins (against God his fellowman and himself), but happy (blessed and fortunate) is he who is kind and merciful to the poor" (proverbs 14:21 AMP). "He who by charging excessive interest and who by unjust efforts to get gain increases his material possession gathers it for him (to spend) who is kind and generous to the poor" (Proverbs 28:8 AMP). "Whoever stops his ears at the cry of the poor will cry out himself and not be heard" (Proverbs 21:13 AMP). "He who has a bountiful eye shall be blessed, for he gives of his bread to the poor" (Proverbs 22:9 AMP). "The Lord blesses everyone who freely gives food to the poor" (Proverbs 22:9 CEV).*

So giving to the poor and needy unlocks the oil of uncommon favor upon one's life. This oil of favor has the capacity to open strange doors of financial opportunity to you. It is a great spiritual factor for financial prosperity. You can't practice it and remain the same!

Another set of people that carries the hidden blessings for financial prosperity are the widows and the fatherless. *". . . and the fatherless and the widows who are in your towns shall come and eat and be satisfied, so that the Lord your God may bless you in all the work of your hands that you do" (Deuteronomy 14:29 AMP). ". . . You must also give food to the poor who live in your town, including orphans, widows and foreigners. If they have enough to eat, then the Lord your God will be pleased and make you successful in everything you do" (Deuteronomy 14:29 CEV).*

I love these scriptures! Nothing frustrates the labor of your hands like being unnecessarily frugal.

At every point in your life, there are those you are better than. God continues to open doors of financial opportunities to those that are channels of blessing to the poor, widows, needy, fatherless, and orphans. These set of people are the heartbeat of God. Therefore, anyone who cares for them is standing in for God; and God will surely pay him back and bless him in return. God owes no man! Once you chose to solve the needs of God—meeting the need of the poor, the widows, the orphans, the fatherless, and the needy (because he cannot come down from heaven to give material things to them except through human hands), God will then decide to make you a divine channel of divine material blessings.

"Caring for the poor is lending to the Lord, and you will be repaid"
(Proverbs 19:17 CEV).

When you show mercy to the needy, poor, widows and orphans, you become qualified to receive mercy too in your days of need. *"Blessed (Happy, to be envied, and spiritually prosperous—with life—joy and satisfaction in God's favor and salvation, regardless of their outward conditions) are the merciful, for they shall obtain mercy" (Matthew 5:7 AMP).*

The Contemporary English Version puts it this way, *"God blesses those people who are merciful. They will be treated with mercy".*

Generosity pays! Whether you are in politics, business, or you are an industrialist, a servant of God (gospel preacher), a working class citizen, generosity pays off, especially in your days of needs and of adversity. Philanthropists can testify of this great truth!

Let's see a man that practiced generosity in his days and see how it affected him:

In Job chapter twenty-nine verse twelve and thirteen, and fifteen to sixteen (Job 29:12, 13, 15, 16), the bible reveals the fundamental reasons for Job's enormous blessings, when he was alive.

". . . because I rescued the poor who cried for help, and the fatherless who had none to assist them. The one who was dying blessed me;

I made the widow's heart to sing. I was eyes to the blind and feet to the lame. I was a father to the needy; I took up the case of a stranger" (NIV).

Job was an unusual Philanthropist! His hands were so free to help the needy. You can imagine why God so blessed him to the point of becoming the envy of his generation!

Read Job 1:1-3. In his time, he was the greatest of all men in the eastern part of the world. You cannot be a giver and not provoke the hidden blessings in the needy (without their knowledge) upon your life! Giving works wonders! *"The liberal soul shall be made fat: and he that watereth shall be watered also himself" (Proverbs 11:25).*

Let us consider the book of Isaiah 58:6-11:

"I'll tell what it really means to worship the Lord. Remove the chains of prisoners who are bound unjustly. Free those who are abused! Share your food with everyone who is hungry; share your home with the poor and homeless. Give cloths to those in need; don't turn away your relatives. Then your light will shine like the dawning sun, and you will quickly be healed. Your honesty will protect you as you advance, and the glory of the Lord will defend you from behind. When you beg the Lord for help, he will answer, "Here I am!" Don't mistreat others or falsely accuse them or say something cruel. Give your food to the hungry and care for the homeless. Then your light will shine in the dark; your darkest hour

will be like the noonday sun. The Lord will always guide you and provide good things to eat when you are in the desert. He will make you healthy. You will be like a garden that has plenty of water or like a stream that never runs dry" (CEV).

From the scriptures above,

1. You will receive an unusual breakthrough (Then shall thy light break forth as the morning—King James Version).
2. You will enjoy divine health. Even if you eventually get sick, you will be healed by the power of God (either by miracle or by medicine). God is faithful!
3. The glory of God (God's power and providence) will protect you from trouble.
4. God will not delay to hear you when you cry for his help in times of trouble
5. You will enjoy divine guidance (divine direction), and you will not be affected by any form of recession, no matter how hard it is for others. Your life will be nourished by divine providence. You will live in plenty in the midst of scarcity.

All these can happen, if you practice the acts mentioned in the above scriptures we just read.

4. **Kingdom investment:** this kind of investment borders on activities done for the promotion of the

gospel in any positive form. It is called, "Kingdom business". Jesus was the first to address the work of God as business. He called it, "My father's business" (Luke 2:49).

The work of God is a massive stock exchange market. It is even too massive to be compared with that of Wall Street in USA. All money market worldwide cannot be compared with the size of God's stock market. And I bet you to it: it pays off absolutely and unarguably!

Nevertheless, how you view God's work determines how you attend to it. Apostle Peter will tell you better (Luke 5:1-7)! He experienced an unusual turn-around, when he had a great net-breaking miracle in his fishing business, after he gave his boat to Jesus to help him stay on the water to preach to the people conveniently. But before then, he toiled all-night and caught nothing, though a professional in fishery business for years.

Times would come when your natural intelligence, experience or professionalism will fail you, but the wisdom of God does not disappoint! Praise God!

To my best of understanding, we are all redeemed to serve God with all our strength, heart and might. We are God's workmanship recreated in Christ Jesus to do God's service (Ephesians 2:10). God is our maker and not we ourselves (Psalms 100:3). We are not only redeemed to live righteously and make it to heaven; we are also redeemed to serve the Lord with all that we have—strength, talent, gift, intellect, money and material possessions here on earth toward the success of the gospel. Those services are called, "Kingdom Investment".

There is no kingdom service that is in vain. God said in his word, *"If they obey and serve him (God), they will spend their days in prosperity and their years in pleasantness and joy"* (Job 36:11 AMP). His word also says, *"You shall serve the Lord your God; He shall bless your bread and water, and I will take sickness from your midst. None shall lose their young by miscarriage or be barren in your land; I will fulfill the number of your days"* (Exodus 23:25, 26 AMP).

God does not forget his true servants indeed! Read the following: *"You have said, It is useless to serve God, and what profit is it, if we keep His ordinances . . ."* (Malachi 3:14). This is what many people are saying against serving in God's kingdom, but God promised to make his true servants his jewels (special possession, peculiar treasure), and to spare them as a man spares his own son who serve him; and also make a difference between those that serve him and those that do not (Malachi 3:17, 18). Any service rendered towards the good of the kingdom of God on earth (whether to his ministers, gospel activities, etc.) will surely reflect on you with God's undeniable blessings here on earth and there eternal (Mark 10:28-30 MSG).

The different ways of investing in God's stock market—kingdom business

1. **Commitment:** this is known as following God's order and seeking the good and promotion of his kingdom (Matthew 6:33). Listen to this: you cannot be fighting against other churches and think that you are promoting God's kingdom. Your denomination alone cannot fulfill the great commission, just as no one member of the body—hand; leg etc. can do all the functions of other members. They all have different functions to deal with. So, please, do your part and wish others well. You are not the one to judge who is truly called or not. Nevertheless, anyone that does believe that Jesus is the Son of God (who came in flesh), and that he was raised from the dead, is of God.

2. **Minding God's project:** Many people thought that paying of kingdom tax (tithe) and giving to the needy are the only way to invest in the kingdom. No! God's kingdom projects are divine avenues to gaining access to divine blessings.

Let's consider these scriptures: *". . . you say this isn't the right time to build a temple for God. But is it right for you to live in expensive houses, while my temple is a pile of ruins? Just look at what's happening. You harvest less than you plant, you never have enough to eat or drink, your cloths don't keep you warm, and your wages are stored in bags full of holes. Think about what I have said! But first, go to the hills and get wood for my temple, so I can take pride in it and be worshipped there. You expected much but received little. And when you brought it home, I made that little disappear. Why have I done this? It's because you hurry up to build your own houses, why my temple is still in ruins. That's also why the dews doesn't fall and harvest fails. And so, at my command everything will become barren—your farmland and pastures, your vineyards and olive trees, your animals and you yourselves. All your hard work will be for nothing" (Haggai 1:2-11 CEV).*

If you read the scriptures above, you would agree with me that some of the struggles or difficulties most Christians are going through today are the result of self-centeredness. They are saved but selfish. Our Christian life and true prosperity sit on 'Love' foundation. If the foundation is faulty, you will live a spiritually barren life; and this will result negatively in the work of your hands.

True love for God and humanity makes one truly free!

The scriptures we just read above did not mention the devil at work. God is the one fighting against the works of their hands here! Though they saved a lot of money, but they later spent it on solving problems. They still lived in scarcity; yet, earning much. They were never really happy. Sometimes, they burrowed to meet up needs, living unfulfilled life. Their businesses kept hitting the rock, facing challenges of all sorts. Even when others were thriving economically, they still faced recession, going back and forth every year. They kept praying and yet got no answer, because the heaven was closed over their head and businesses. Where others gained favor, they were faced with disappointment in return, and much more to mention.

Any time you back God's project off, God backs you off too. You cannot reap where you did not sow. Budgeting for God's project provokes a divine budget for your life and endeavor. God will surely continue to look over your life and business or job to see to your success.

There was a time in the history of the Jews in the land of Israel, when God's ark was returned from the land of the Philistine. King David, out of fear, refused to have anything to do with ark, seeing that Uzzah, the son of Abinadab, died trying to rescue the ark from falling. Then, King David ordered that the ark should be put in the house of Obededom, the Gittite. Obededom kept the ark and in three months, God prospered the house of Obededom so much that it was so obvious. Such prosperity could only be by God's help and favor. When King Divid saw it, he commanded that the ark be brought to his house. What an envy God can make you be to your generation when you are concerned about Him! Read 1 Chronicles 13:1-14.

You cannot take care of God's business and not prosper!

Let us not be like the rich young fool, who became very wealthy and was not concerned about God's work, and God took his life in the middle of his age (Luke 12:15-21). This story is a true evidence that giving is living!

You need to keep giving to the advancement of the kingdom of God here on earth. Give to God's work in any form—to the work of evangelism of souls into the kingdom of God, to the building of Christian worship centers (Church buildings), or to any church project. Advancing the kingdom of God means advancing your life!

5. **Honoring your biological parent:** I have taken observations of the lifestyle of Asians; and I have discovered that one of their greatest secrets for success is respect for the elders or their parents. Although, some among them do this as a result of fear that the ghost of their parents will harass them (if they don't care and respect their parents), some others have learned this act of respect from the teaching of Buddha. Nevertheless, this idea is divine and scriptural. It provokes divine blessings upon the children.

The bible teaches us to honor our father and mother, because it is the first commandment to have a promise attached to it. The promise is that an obedient child will live long on earth, and it will be well with the child

(Ephesians 6:2, 3). That is to say that the child will carry a provoked blessing from God, through his/her parent, to succeed in life.

What a promise! The word of God is the revelation of truth, no matter who is in doubt of it. God cannot lie!

I heard of a story of a certain young lady, who could not give birth to a child after about two years of marriage. She heard this great truth for the first time in her life, and she made her way to visit her mother after two years of a prolonged enmity between both of them. When she finally apologized to her mother and gave her a mind-provoking present, her mother blessed her from her heart, and that same month, she got pregnant miraculously. What a great story! Revelation of truth like this one is a blessing itself!

You cannot break a divine law and go away with it. Your dishonor to your biological parent will always play a negative role in your life. (Please, note that your parent are not the custodian of your destiny. They are only given the privilege to raise you and care for you, but not to choose your destiny for you. If you must also succeed in your career, you must be able to follow your passion).

See what the bible says about children and parents: *"Whoso curseth his father or mother, his lamp shall be put out in obscure darkness" (Proverbs 20:20).* The contemporary English

Version puts it this way, *"Children who curse their parents will go to the land of darkness long before their time"*. Amplified Version says, *"Whoever curses his father or his mother, his lamp shall be put out in complete darkness"*.

How can one walk in darkness and still prosper? The negative forces of life will keep a great chase at such a person. Life will keep singing the songs of misfortune in such person's life. It will really not be well with him/her. May God deliver such person from now on as they read this great truth in Jesus' name!

To thread against divine laws is to fight against true success. You need to have a great value and respect for your parents. In their mouths lie hidden divine blessings that you do not know about. Provoke it for your good!

For those of you in Africa that have parents that are involved in witchcraft practices (who use this medium to bewitch their children), just connect to God's covenant and God will handle the rest for you.

Honoring your parent gladdens their hearts. When you honor your parents with respect and care, they will bless you from the depth of their hearts. That is the kind of blessing that really works! Remember Isaac and his children when he was about to die (Genesis 27:1-41)!

You may still prosper while dishonoring your family (because they may be praying good prayers for you out of parental care) but it is possible that you may not live long enough to enjoy your hard-earned wealth. Be wise!

6. **Humility and the fear of the Lord:** a truly humble person lives by the dictates of God's word. The fear of God opens the door to a three-fold blessing—riches, honor and life. Life here means true happiness, fulfillment and eternal satisfaction, and longevity. *"By humility and the fear of the Lord are riches, and honor, and life" (Proverbs 22:4).*

Ill-gotten wealth does not come with long life and true satisfaction! Know this! So, I am not talking about ill-gotten wealth here.

Humility pays! *"A man's pride will bring him low, but he who is of a humble spirit will obtain honor" (Proverbs 29:23).*

Grace (favor and divine ability) is only accessible to the humble, but God resists the proud (James 4:6). Humble people easily get help and favor, but proud people naturally build walls of disfavor and resistance around themselves. If you really want to make headway, you must wear the garment of true humility in your spirit. This is why loyalists excel more than those that rate themselves higher than they really are.

Humility is the true or correct estimation of oneself. Meanwhile, it takes wisdom to discern the difference between pride and humility. Read my book, "Fulfilling your destiny with ease". Even in companies or organizations, humble people rise faster than proud people. Pride creates a limit around its victims, no matter how gifted they are. Be wise and humble yourself!

7. **Honoring God with your first fruit:** God said in Malachi 1:4, ". . . if I then be a father, where is my honor?"

One of the ways to honor God is to give him the best or quality offering from your income or produce from your farm, if you are a farmer (Proverbs 3:9, 10). The reward for doing that is that your storage (bank account) will be filled with plenty, and you will enjoy unending blessings and favor.

God has vowed to honor those that honor him (1 Samuel 2:30), and he keeps His word (Psalms 89:34).

Honoring God is not even an option but a command! Whether you are a business person, a merchant or a civil servant, you need to adopt the habit of honoring God with your material substances.

8. **Diligence:** the word 'Diligence' means hard work or perspiration. It means total commitment to your assignment in life, with a determination for completion.

To embark on what divinity did not wire or design you for is to sign up for frustration or disillusionment in the future, as confusion will soon begin its journey of enslaving your psyche. Nothing gives life a meaning or flavor like making a living out of what we call hobby! It is absolutely satisfying and fulfilling! You need to discover what God has really wired you to do in your lifetime. Your abilities and talent are designed in you to fulfill a mission on earth.

So, laboring for what you have no passion for is to reduce your life span. Imagine trying to drive an automobile (car with tires) in an ocean or sailing a boat on the land! It is nothing but a suicidal and an impossible mission in disguise! Many people in this world are already involved in activities that are frustrating their energy and mental prowess. You will only be at your best when you are involved in something that unlocks your inner capacity, energy and wisdom.

Nevertheless, diligence is really good when it has to do with what you love to do best in your life. It is a divine principle for success. Purpose (your assignment in life) plus diligence (hard work) in service to humanity equals success!

The Contemporary English Version says, *"Hard work is worthwhile, but empty talk will make you poor" (proverbs 14:23).*

Lazy people will always remain servants to those that are diligent. They only dream dreams but the diligent ones transmute their dreams to reality. I love to keep having dreams, but I also love to see to it that my dreams come true.

The bible says, *"The desire of the slothful killeth him, for his hands refuse to labor" (Proverbs 21:25)*. It also says, *"He becometh poor that dealeth with a slack hand: but the hand of the diligent maketh rich" (Proverbs 10:4)*.

I define work as a means of translating one's dream into its physical reality. Without work, dreams die unfulfilled! Work reveals your true self to your generation. Nobody really knows what you worth until diligence is employed in service.

A wise man said, "Work as if everything depends on you; pray as if everything depends on God!"

God has a responsibility to help you in life, but you also have a responsibility to make your life what you want it to be. God's job in your life is focused on the humanly-impossible issues, while your job is to follow his instructions and focus on the humanly-possible issues. God cannot do your job for you. For example, God is giving me inspirations, while I do the writing. God cannot do for you what you can do for yourself! Imagine asking God to eat for you! That is insanity!

Greatness lies in everyone, but the act of diligence brings it out (Proverbs 22:29)!

Be diligent to make your dream come true! It really pays off!

9. **Remain just before God:** it pays to be just! To be just means living by the standard of God's word.

Righteousness is a spiritual catalyst for provoking the blessings of God! *"The wealth of the sinners are laid up for the just" (Proverbs 13:22).* God cannot lie! One way or the other, this happens!

Divine wealth is connected to righteousness. Remember Job (Job 1:1-3)! It is possible to be just and still be wealthy. If Job was, anybody can, if such person walk in righteousness!

So, let us cultivate the habit of pleasing God always! It pays to do so!

Welcome to the top

As you put the principles you have just learned from this book to work, may your life reflect God's goodness more than you ever imagined! May you fly high without boundaries in your life!

Welcome to the place of great fulfillment and wealth! God bless you real good!

ABOUT THE AUTHOR

Prophet Harrison I. Enudi is the President of Destiny Awareness Outreach (A non-denominational ministry). He is a teacher of God's word, and an author with over 14,000 readers on Scribd.com. His life and ministry has really been a blessing and an inspiration to many people around the world, especially in United State, African and Asian continent.

His ministry borders around the teaching of 'Destiny', 'Success', 'Marriage', and 'The Supernatural'. As a Prophet, he also operate in the prophetic with healing and deliverance anointing. He is a man being sort for in regards to seminars, conferences and various church programs. He graduated from Portable Bible School located in Kaduna, Nigeria; and also, from Word of Faith Bible Institute, Lagos, Nigeria.

Prophet Harrison is a divine instrument for bringing a transformation in the lives of people, healing to the sick, revival to the body of Christ, bringing people into their destinies, and for helping the children of God to discover their full spiritual ability and capacity in Christ, in order to help them keep the devil under their control, be in charge of their destinies, spiritual environment, and all forms of situation that emerges around their lives. He is this end-time divine instrument for the raising of champions and spiritual leaders in Christ.

Also, he is the author of two life-changing books titled, "Fulfilling your destiny with ease" and "Expressing the supernatural". The books were published is the United States of America, and are being marketed worldwide, especially through the biggest online bookstores—Amazon.com, borders.com, and barnesandnoble.com.

Please, visit his website at www.pastorharrisonenudi.org.